90 DAYS OF BREAKTHROUGH

POWERFUL DECLARATIONS FOR A MIRACULOUS LIFE

KYNAN BRIDGES

90 DAYS OF BREAKTHROUGH

POWERFUL DECLARATIONS FOR A MIRACULOUS LIFE

WHITAKER HOUSE

Boldface type in the Scripture quotations indicates the author's emphasis. The forms LORD and GOD (in small capital letters) in Bible quotations represent the Hebrew name for God *Yahweh* (Jehovah), while *Lord* and *God* normally represent the name *Adonai*, in accordance with the Bible version used.

90 DAYS OF BREAKTHROUGH:
POWERFUL DECLARATIONS FOR A MIRACULOUS LIFE

Kynan Bridges Ministries, Inc.
P.O. Box 159 | Ruskin, FL 33575
www.kynanbridges.com
info@kynanbridges.com

ISBN: 979-8-88769-239-5
Printed in the United States of America

Whitaker House
1030 Hunt Valley Circle | New Kensington, PA 15068
www.whitakerhouse.com

Library of Congress Control Number for hardcover edition: https://lccn.loc.gov/2020300395

1 2 3 4 5 6 7 8 9 10 11 **w** 31 30 29 28 27 26 25 24

Contents

Day 1: Cast Your Net on the *Right* Side

And [Jesus] *said to them, Cast the net on the right side of the ship, and you shall find. They cast therefore, and now they were not able to draw it for the multitude of fishes.*
(John 21:6)

My dad was an avid fisherman, and I remember going fishing with him frequently as a kid, spending more time on the lake than most people I knew. Early on, I realized that fishing was a very technical activity. For example, knowing *where* to cast your line made all the difference. That is why my dad would move to several locations on the lake throughout the day.

We can learn a valuable spiritual lesson from the practice of fishing at the right location, as we see in the following incidents involving Jesus and His disciples. After His resurrection, Jesus encountered the disciples fishing in the Sea of Galilee and asked them a very interesting question: *"Children, have you any meat?"* (John 21:5). They told Him they had none. In the Bible, "meat" represents provision or sustenance. Whether we realize it or not, God is interested in the level of provision you and I enjoy. Like any good Father, He wants us to "eat well" in all areas of our lives. Jesus told Peter and the other disciples to cast their net on the *right* side of the ship in order to obtain a catch of fish. If there is a "right" side, there must also be a "wrong" side. The moment Peter cast the net on the right side, they caught more fish than they had ever caught before. That is the power of obeying a divine instruction.

A similar incident occurred early in Jesus's ministry, just before Peter, James, and John became His disciples. After teaching the crowds, Jesus told Peter, "*Launch out into the deep, and let down your nets for a draught*" (Luke 5:4). Peter's initial response was, "*We have* [already] *toiled all the night*" (verse 5), but he added, "*Nevertheless at Your word I will let down the net*" (verse 5). Have you ever felt like you were toiling all day and all night—or all week, all month, or all year—and yet were seeing few results? Or maybe no results at all? Though the disciples had been doing a lot of fishing (working), they hadn't been doing it God's way; they had been doing it in their own strength. But when they followed Jesus's instruction, they caught so many fish that their net broke. (See verse 6.)

As happened for Peter, one instruction from the Lord can transform your life. The key to experiencing supernatural breakthrough is making the decision to wholeheartedly obey God's Word. When you do, then you, too, will see a supernatural harvest in your life.

Day 1: BREAKTHROUGH PRAYER

Father, in the name of Jesus, I declare that I walk in perfect obedience to Your divine instruction. I declare that Your provision flows in every area of my life. Doors of supernatural grace are open to me, and I experience unusual success in every area of my life. Things that were difficult before have become easy. Divine multiplication manifests in my life as I release my faith in Your Word and act on Your instruction. Things are changing for me right now. In the name of Jesus, amen!

Day 2: Willing and Obedient

If you be willing and obedient, you shall eat the good of the land. (Isaiah 1:19)

My seventh-grade teacher, Ms. Green, frequently taught her class about the value of obedience. One day, she told us a story of a little girl who was playing out in the yard while her grandmother was sitting on the porch. The grandmother suddenly yelled at the little girl, "Stop!" so she froze in her tracks. Then the grandmother said, "Now, turn around and walk this way!" The little girl quickly complied with these instructions, turning around and walking toward her grandmother until she arrived on the porch. Her grandmother pointed out at the yard and said, "Look!" As the girl turned and looked, she saw a copperhead snake right near the place where she had been playing. If she had hesitated to obey her grandmother for one second, it could have cost her life.

This is a striking illustration of the value of obeying trusted authority. How much more important is it for us to obey our heavenly Father? Often, we underestimate the value of obedience in the kingdom of God, but it is a key factor in experiencing supernatural breakthrough. The Bible says, *"If you be willing and obedient, you shall eat the good of the land."* This is true for every area of our lives. Yes, we are under the grace of God, and He forgives us when we sin, but nothing can replace obedience. As we obey God, we posture ourselves to walk in His highest and best for our lives. On the other hand, if we disobey God, we remove ourselves from the abundant harvest He has for us.

The word *"willing"* in Isaiah 1:19 comes from the Hebrew word *abah*, among whose meanings is "to consent, yield to, accept." Just as the young lady yielded to her grandmother, we must consciously and consistently yield to the Word of God. The word *"obedient"* here comes from the Hebrew word *shama*, which means "to hear, listen to, obey." We must listen to and obey what God instructs us; the sooner we heed what God tells us to do, the sooner we will prosper. The Bible admonishes us to be both hearers and doers of the Word. (See James 1:22.) As we obey God, we will enjoy *"the good of the land."*

Day 2: BREAKTHROUGH PRAYER

Father, in the name of Jesus, Your Word says that if we are willing and obedient, we will eat the good of the land. I declare that I walk in obedience to Your Word. Romans 10:17 says, *"Faith comes by hearing, and hearing by the word of God."* As I hear Your word, I respond in faith and obedience to Your instruction. "Your sheep hear Your voice, and a stranger they will not follow"; I am one of Your sheep; therefore, I hear Your voice clearly, and I will not follow the voice of a stranger. I declare that I enjoy the good of the land in every area of my life. In Jesus's name, amen! (See John 10:1–5.)

Day 3: Breakthroughs Come Suddenly

And suddenly there was a great earthquake, so that the foundations of the prison were shaken: and immediately all the doors were opened, and every one's bands were loosed.

(Acts 16:26)

Are you ready for your "suddenly" breakthrough? In the book of Acts, Paul and Silas were in prison, and the Bible says that as they prayed and sang, "*suddenly there was a great earthquake*" that shook the foundations of the jail, opened the cell doors, and released everyone's shackles. The dictionary defines *suddenly* as "quickly and unexpectedly." Even though Paul and Silas were praying, they did not know that God would deliver them with such power, speed, and magnitude. This is what a "suddenly" is all about.

Suddenly means that no one will be expecting the miracle to take place in the way that it does. Suddenly means that the doors will swing open so fast and wide that it will cause an "earthquake." When suddenly takes place, natural limitations are dissolved, and time is interrupted by eternity. The laws of delay and stagnation are broken.

Are you ready for a suddenly? God is turning your midnight into a suddenly, in Jesus's name! I declare that your "suddenly season" is upon you now! It doesn't matter how long you may have been in bondage or captivity, God is about to show up in your life in a magnanimous way. You are about to see foundations shaken, doors opened, and shackles loosed.

Day 3: BREAKTHROUGH PRAYER

Father, in the name of Jesus, I declare that my suddenly season is here. I declare that doors open miraculously and all chains are broken off my life. The things that were difficult in the past will not be difficult anymore because of the working of Your supernatural power. Walls come down and doors swing open for me, right now! I am a believer in Your Word; therefore, I release my faith for miracles now. I declare that every work of the enemy that has been operating in my life is destroyed by the power of the Holy Spirit. I declare that praise is my weapon, and I use this weapon to push back the enemy. I take authority over every weapon of the enemy fashioned against me, in Jesus's name. Amen! (See Isaiah 54:17.)

Day 4: The Beautiful Gate

And a certain man lame from his mother's womb was carried, whom they laid daily at the gate of the temple which is called Beautiful, to ask alms of them that entered into the temple. (Acts 3:2)

You have probably heard the story about the paralyzed man at the Beautiful Gate of the temple in Jerusalem. (See Acts 3:1–10.) This paralysis affected every area of his life, including his livelihood—his affliction had resulted in his becoming a beggar. I can imagine the pain and embarrassment this man experienced daily. I believe he represents many people in the church today (as well as millions of others throughout the world). The thing about pain is that it doesn't discriminate. Young or old, rich or poor, we have all experienced some sort of pain in our lives. And each of us can relate to some form of paralysis, whether spiritual, emotional, financial, or physical—and whether that paralysis is in the past or the present.

This man had been made into a beggar because of his pain. He was trapped in a cycle of defeat, and he had been conditioned to settle for less than God's best for his life. It was not God's will for him to live in that condition. Little did he know that he was about to have a beautiful, life-changing day by an encounter with Peter and John and the power of the resurrected Christ, through which he was healed of his infirmity. The Bible says, *"Beautiful for situation, the joy of the whole earth, is mount Zion, on the sides of the north, the city of the great King"* (Psalm 48:2).

As He did for the paralyzed man, God is about to grant you a beautiful day, turning your situation around for His glory. Your life will never be the same again, in Jesus's name!

Day 4: BREAKTHROUGH PRAYER

Father, in the matchless name of Jesus, I declare that You are beautiful in every situation of my life. According to John 10:10, Jesus came that I might have life and have it more abundantly; therefore, I declare that I possess an abundant life in Christ Jesus. I am not a prisoner of pain, but by the grace of God, I am liberated from all shackles of defeat and victimhood. Spiritual, physical, mental, and emotional paralysis have no place in my life. I rise up in faith and bold confidence in the Word of God and possess the promises that You, Father, have so graciously prepared for me and my family. My life will flourish, increase, and multiply according to Your purpose and plan. I will never be the same again. In the name of Jesus, amen!

Day 5: The Power of Decrees

You shall also decree a thing, and it shall be established to you: and the light shall shine upon your ways. (Job 22:28)

"*You shall also decree a thing, and it shall be established.*" Whether you realize it or not, words are extremely powerful. Every word we speak has a substantial and residual effect in our lives and the lives of others. Many Christians have never truly understood the power of their words, and this is one of the reasons why they use their words so carelessly. What if I told you that everything you said would become a reality? What would you say and what would you refrain from saying?

Our words shape the world we live in. This is the underlying spiritual principle behind making faith proclamations. The Hebrew word for "*decree*" in Job 22:28 is *gazar,* which means, among other things, "to cut, divide, cut down, or cut off." A decree is an official order that holds legal authority and has the ability to cut off that which is illegal. When we make spiritual decrees, we are invoking God's law. The Bible says, "*Whatsoever you shall bind on earth shall be bound in heaven: and whatsoever you shall loose on earth shall be loosed in heaven*" (Matthew 18:18). Jesus has given us authority, and this authority is released through decrees and declarations. When we make a faith-filled decree according to the Word of God, we are releasing the authority and power of heaven into the earth, and what we decree will be established. The word "*established*" in the verse from Job is *quwm*, among whose meanings are "to rise, arise, stand, rise up, stand up." What we decree will arise.

Today, God is waiting for you to decree *His* Word into your life and the lives of your loved ones. Nothing happens until you release the decree. Speak God's Word in faith, and watch the heavens open.

Day 5: BREAKTHROUGH PRAYER

Father, Your Word says that whatever I bind on earth will be bound in heaven, and whatever I loose on earth will be loosed in heaven; therefore, I declare that all satanic activity operating in my life is broken and released in the name of Jesus. I decree that Your authority operates in and through me, and as a result of this reality, sickness, disease, and poverty have to flee from me. I decree that all curses in my life are broken, and that Your healing power is brought into manifestation right now. In the name of Jesus, amen.

Day 6: Take It by Force

And from the days of John the Baptist until now the kingdom of heaven suffers violence, and the violent take it by force. (Matthew 11:12)

I hear people say things like, "God will do it, if it is His will!" Yes, God will perform His will, but when it comes to experiencing supernatural breakthrough in line with His will, there is no room for passivity. The Bible says that "*the kingdom of heaven suffers violence, and the violent take it by force.*" Another translation says, in effect, "They violently press in to it."

You will not experience supernatural breakthrough in your life until you learn to press in to God's promises. Just because you are experiencing difficulty or opposition doesn't mean that God has forgotten you or hasn't heard your prayers. In fact, it often means quite the opposite; you may be experiencing spiritual resistance to the answer. Jesus said, "*Therefore I say to you, What things soever you desire, when you pray, believe that you receive them, and you shall have them*" (Mark 11:24). We must "*believe that* [we] *receive them.*" The Greek word translated "*receive*" is *lambanō*, among whose meanings is "to take in order to carry away." The word picture is of a person taking something valuable to themselves as a prized possession. Simply put, when you pray, take what belongs to you. Lay hold of it! And don't let it go. Don't sit back and wait passively. Make up your mind today that if God promised it to you, then it belongs to you. Your life will take a drastic turn the moment you make up your mind to no longer accept defeat as an option.

Day 6: BREAKTHROUGH PRAYER

Father, in the name of Jesus, I thank You for who You are and all that You have done in my life. Your Word is pregnant with miracle power; therefore, I declare Your Word over every area of my life. I lay hold of Your promises by faith, and I decree that I have already received what You have spoken. I declare that I persevere against all spiritual opposition and demonic resistance in my life and in the lives of those for whom I am praying. I will not sit back and watch my life pass by; instead, I will appropriate Your promises by faith in the Word of God. In Jesus's name, amen.

Day 7: Operation Jericho

And the Lord *said to Joshua, See, I have given into your hand Jericho, and the king thereof, and the mighty men of valor.* (Joshua 6:2)

Jericho was known for its fortified walls. For the Israelites, Jericho was the barrier between them and the promised land. For us, the walls of Jericho represent the limitations that so many of us have experienced at various points in this journey called life.

It is important to remember that walls are built for only two purposes: to keep something out or to keep something in. How many areas of your life have been surrounded by walls? How many times has God promised you something, and all of a sudden, you faced spiritual opposition or resistance? You, my friend, are a prime candidate for an "Operation Jericho" mission. It is time to bring those walls down! The biggest breakthrough you have ever seen or experienced is just beyond the walls of opposition and limitation. God is calling you to experience so much more!

If you truly realized that your greatest blessing was closer to you than it has ever been, would you be willing to give up so easily? I am sure the answer is, "Absolutely not!" The enemy of your soul knows that you are about to experience breakthrough like you can't even imagine; therefore, he has attempted to hit you with everything he can. However, I have good news for you—he has failed miserably! That wall in front of your future blessings is coming down; all you have to do is believe God's Word and keep moving forward. Keep marching toward the promise! Keep declaring God's faithfulness and shouting His praises, and suddenly you will see victory.

Day 7: BREAKTHROUGH PRAYER

Father, in the name of Jesus, I thank You for Your faithfulness in every area of my life. Thank You for launching an "Operation Jericho" mission over my life and destiny. I boldly declare that no weapon formed against me will be able to prosper. Nothing will stand in my or in the way of my breakthrough. I declare that You, Lord, are good and Your mercy endures forever. I declare that all hindrances, blockages, and barriers are broken right now, in the name of Jesus. As I move forward in faith, I thank You for bold confidence and enhanced spiritual eyesight that enables me to recognize and yield to Your mighty hand working in my life. In Jesus's name, amen! (See Isaiah 54:17; Psalm 100:5; 106:1; 118:29.)

Day 8: Double Portion

For your shame you shall have double; and for confusion they shall rejoice in their portion: therefore in their land they shall possess the double: everlasting joy shall be to them. (Isaiah 61:7)

Whenever I went to the ice cream shop as a boy, I always wanted a double scoop. There was just something about knowing I was getting "extra" that made it more exciting. As the saying goes, "The more the merrier." Well, that adage is more spiritual than you may realize. God is a God of more than enough. One of the names for God is El Shaddai, which literally means, "almighty, most powerful." The Lord bountifully supplies. And He rewards those who diligently seek Him with their whole hearts. (See Hebrews 11:6.)

But I have even greater news for you. The Word of God promises that in exchange for your shame, you will receive a double blessing. In other words, God is about to give you double for your trouble. The prophet Elisha asked for a "*double portion*" of the anointing that was on the life of his mentor, Elijah, and God honored his request. (See 2 Kings 2:9–14.) Furthermore, the Bible says that Job received double after his affliction. (See Job 42:10.) Don't settle for "just enough" when we serve a God who longs to pour out more and more. I believe that you are going to receive a double portion of grace, favor, and anointing upon your life as you seek God with your whole heart.

God is a God of double! The question is, Are you ready to receive? Religious tradition has taught us that we are supposed to be modest and not ask for much, but this is not what the Bible tells us to do. Jesus said, *"Ask, and you shall receive, that your joy may be full"* (John 16:24). God wants us to be full to overflowing. This is the abundant life that Jesus came to give us, according to John 10:10. Are you ready to receive a double portion in every area of your life?

Day 8: BREAKTHROUGH PRAYER

Father, in the name of Jesus, I recognize that You are God Almighty. You are my all-sufficient source of everything good and beneficial, and I declare that Your goodness overflows in my life and family. I desire the abundant life that You have graciously provided for me. I refuse to settle for "just enough" when You, Father, are the God of more than enough! In Jesus's name, amen!

Day 9: Spirit of Prevention

Wherefore we would have come to you, even I Paul, once and again; but Satan hindered us.

(1 Thessalonians 2:18)

I am no stranger to spiritual opposition. In fact, in the first several years of my ministry, I received intense, on-the-job training in the area of spiritual warfare. Here is one of the lessons I learned during that season of my life: the greater the promises and the blessings, the greater the spiritual opposition to keep you from receiving those promises and blessings.

I well remember a particular time when things just didn't seem to be working out for my family. I had a successful book project, but then, out of nowhere, our finances dried up. It didn't make any sense! Eventually, God revealed to me and my wife that this was a "spirit of prevention." A spirit of prevention is a form of opposition—spiritual or physical—that has been designed to keep you from receiving what God has promised you or to prevent you from fulfilling the assignment God has given you. Paul the apostle seems to have had one or two run-ins with this spirit. In 1 Thessalonians 2:18, he wrote, "*Wherefore we would have come to you...; but Satan hindered us.*"

The Hebrew word for Satan, *śāṭān,* means "adversary," or "one who withstands." Another definition I have come across is "one who hinders the path of another." The purpose of a spirit of prevention is to frustrate and discourage you. The prophet Daniel learned that the answer to one of his prayers had been delayed by such a spirit. It was revealed to him that his prayer had been heard the very moment he prayed, but the reply was hindered by the *"prince of the kingdom of Persia"*—a demonic entity. (See Daniel 10:1–14.) Once you recognize the activity of a spirit of prevention, you can break its power through prayer and intercession.

Day 9: BREAKTHROUGH PRAYER

Father, in the name of Jesus, I thank You that You have given me the authority to pray against the spirit of prevention. I thank You that You hear me when I pray, and You immediately move on my behalf. You have given me *"power to tread on serpents and scorpions, and over all the power of the enemy,"* and nothing will by any means hurt me. I move forward in the power of Your Word, and I declare that Satan cannot frustrate or hinder me. Father, I thank You that my prayers have already been answered and that Your ministering angels have cleared the path for breakthrough. I receive the promises and blessings You have sent me. I declare that Satan has no power over me or my situation. He cannot stop what God has for me. Any prevention tactics organized against me must leave my life right now, in the name of Jesus. Amen! (See Luke 10:19.)

Day 10: Take Authority over the Spirit of Fear

For God has not given us the spirit of fear; but of power, and of love, and of a sound mind. (2 Timothy 1:7)

The Bible is very clear that God has not given us a spirit of fear, but rather of power, love, and a sound mind. Notice that the writer of 2 Timothy referred to fear as a "*spirit*." Moreover, the Greek word translated "*fear*" in the above verse means "timidity," "fearfulness," or "cowardice." God has not called you and me to be timid or fearful—He has called us to be bold! The Bible actually says, "*The righteous are bold as a lion*" (Proverbs 28:1).

What are you afraid of today? What is the enemy using to intimidate you? Whatever it is, it is time to take authority over it. In other words, God wants you to take courage. Courage is not always the absence of fear; it is often the willingness to move forward *in the face of fear*. When we are courageous, we are telling fear, "You have no power over me!" Whether it's a negative report from the doctor, a failed marriage, unruly children, or anything else, God is more than able to bring you through it. Do not be afraid; God is with you! It is time for you to stand on His Word and watch Him bring you into the manifestation of what He has promised for your life.

Day 10: BREAKTHROUGH PRAYER

Father, Your Word declares that You have not given me a spirit of fear, but of power, love, and a sound mind.

Therefore, I declare that no weapon formed against me will prosper. I refuse to cower in the face of fear, and I refuse to be manipulated by my emotions. I will not allow what I see to control my life. I am not moved by what I see. I am not moved by what I hear. I am moved only by the Word of God. I declare that I have faith and confidence in God's Word. In Jesus's name, amen! (See Isaiah 54:17.)

Day 11: Stop Making Excuses

I can do all things through Christ which strengthens me.
(Philippians 4:13)

The Bible records that when Adam was confronted by God about his sin of disobedience, he blamed his wife, saying, in effect, "It was the fault of the woman You gave me!" (See Genesis 3:11–12.) Unfortunately, I can relate to Adam's defensiveness. There was a season in my life when I was a professional blame-shifter. A blame-shifter is someone who does not take responsibility for their mistakes or their problems, but instead puts the blame on someone or something else. Many people in the body of Christ have adopted this attitude. They blame their lack of success on the circumstances in which they were raised. They blame their parents for not being there for them. They blame their spouses for not being loving enough. Yet the moment we are born again, all such excuses become obsolete. Why? Because the Bible says we can do all things through Christ who strengthens us.

The name *Christ* means "anointed." Therefore, we can do all things through the Anointed One and His anointing. I want you to understand that, as a believer, the anointing of the Holy Spirit is upon you and in you. As a result, there is no barrier big enough to prevent you from fulfilling your destiny in God.

So, stop making excuses! Stop allowing the circumstances of your life to dictate what you can and can't have, and how far you can go. You can go as far as God says you can go, and you can have as much as God says you can have. The moment you decide that you will never make another excuse in your life, but will instead rely on God's grace and power, is the moment you will begin to see exponential increase. You can do all things through Christ who strengthens you. Now, act like it!

Day 11: BREAKTHROUGH PRAYER

Father, Your Word declares, *"I can do all things through Christ which strengthens me."* Therefore, I boldly declare that nothing can stand in the way of the fulfillment of my destiny. No matter what the circumstances into which I was born, the difficult situations I have encountered in life, or the pain I have experienced, I refuse to be a victim. *Victimhood* is not in my vocabulary. Jesus never took on a victim attitude. Therefore, I will never take on a victim mentality. In the name of Jesus, I reject any thought or suggestion that attempts to victimize me. I possess an anointing from God that enables me to overcome every challenge or difficulty that comes my way. I declare that I possess the mind of Christ. I pull down every thought or imagination of victimhood or failure in my life, in the name of Jesus. I can do all things through Christ who gives me strength. In Jesus's name, amen! (See 1 Corinthians 2:16; 2 Corinthians 10:5.)

Day 12: No More Delay!

For He will finish the work, and cut it short in righteousness: because a short work will the Lord make upon the earth. (Romans 9:28)

Let me be honest with you: there's probably nothing I hate more than traffic! Many times, when I am driving in stop-and-go traffic, I try to figure out the reason for the delay. Often, it turns out there's an accident on the other side of the road or highway, and people have slowed down to see what's happening. Traffic congestion is never fun, because it keeps us from getting to our destination at the time we are scheduled to arrive—or at the time we *want* to arrive.

Natural delays are not much different from spiritual delays. There are many people in the body of Christ right now who are experiencing unnecessary delays in their lives and destinies. The Israelites in the book of Exodus were unnecessarily delayed—their trip to the promised land was supposed to be a two-week journey, but it took them forty years because of their disobedience to God. Talk about a delay!

You might be experiencing a delay in your life or ministry right now. You are not where you thought you would be by this point. Maybe things haven't worked out the way you thought they would. I have great news for you—God is a God of breakthrough, and He knows how to accelerate your destiny. If you have been disobedient to Him, repent and ask Him to forgive you and to work out His purposes in your life. Keep holding on to God's promises in faith.

One time, I was scheduled to preach on the West Coast and my flight was delayed by two hours. This was a serious problem because I would be late for the conference at which I was the keynote speaker. While we were in flight, I fell asleep, and when I woke up, we were already descending. I looked at my watch (which I had already set ahead), and I realized that the plane was landing on time. How could that be? It turns out that the pilot took a faster route to get there. Likewise, I believe that God is about to accelerate you, despite any previous delays you may have experienced in your life. Let go of the past—and move forward!

Day 12: BREAKTHROUGH PRAYER

Father, in the name of Jesus, I recognize that You are the Lord of the breakthrough. You are loving and faithful, and Your Word is from everlasting to everlasting. Therefore, I declare that I have stepped into a season of acceleration. Despite my failures and mistakes, and regardless of any past delays, I know that You are more than able to get me where You have called me to be. I will not waste unnecessary time dwelling on past failures, but I will make a conscious decision today to move forward in Your grace and abundant favor. I receive the accelerated manifestation of answers to prayers, prophetic words, blessings, open doors, and opportunities. I declare that my life is on track and scheduled for predestined arrival. In the name of Jesus, amen!

Day 13: The Biology of Belief

Faith comes by hearing, and hearing by the word of God.
(Romans 10:17)

My mother was a biology and chemistry teacher for nearly twenty-five years. In a way, her vocation created significant challenges for me when I was growing up because I was not allowed to get low marks in those particular subjects! Can you imagine failing a biology class when your mother is a biology teacher?

Yet as I studied these subjects, I had no idea that learning biology and chemistry would provide a foundation for my understanding of the spiritual realm. The Bible says that "*faith comes by hearing, and hearing by the word of God.*" Faith is a living spiritual "organ," and just like a physical organ, it must be nourished or it will die. And our faith is fed by what we allow into our ear gates.

Therefore, what—and whom—are you listening to? What you hear, and the way you hear it, will ultimately determine the level and maturity of your faith. Do you listen to the *doubting Thomas* playing over the radio or on the Internet? Do you surround yourself with friends who don't possess the same degree of faith and expectancy that you do? Do you constantly listen to news reports that feed your fear and speculation? All these things are faith-killers. But the Word of God builds our faith. If you want to improve your spiritual—and even your physical—health, you must change your spiritual diet to take in more of the Word. For example, if there are stubborn obstacles in front of your God-given purpose, nourish yourself with Philippians 4:13. If there are symptoms of sickness in your body, feast on 1 Peter 2:24. As you do so, your faith will become strong, mature, and resilient against temporal setbacks and the attacks of the enemy.

Day 13: BREAKTHROUGH PRAYER

Father, in the name of Jesus, Your Word declares that "*faith comes by hearing. and hearing by the word of God.*" Therefore, I declare that my faith is strong. I feast on a healthy diet of the Word of God, and the fruit of my diet is bold confidence in Your Word. The Bible says that "*faith is the substance of things hoped for, the evidence of things not seen.*" Therefore, I declare that I possess supernatural faith. I refuse to give in to doubt or fear. I refuse to feed on spiritual junk food. I declare that, in You, my faith is flourishing and growing. Faith causes me to look beyond my natural circumstances and to hold on to the truth of Your Word. In Jesus's name, amen! (See Hebrews 11:1.)

Day 14: Obey the Word

If you will diligently hearken to the voice of the LORD your God, and will do that which is right in His sight, and will give ear to His commandments, and keep all His statutes, I will put none of these diseases upon you, which I have brought upon the Egyptians: for I am the LORD that heals you. (Exodus 15:26)

One of the most underestimated spiritual principles in the church today is that obedience keeps us in right relationship with God and in position to receive His blessings. The prophet Samuel told King Saul, "*To obey is better than sacrifice*" (1 Samuel 15:22). If only we would learn the value and blessing of obedience! The Bible tells us clearly that if we are willing and obedient, we will eat the good of the land. (See Isaiah 1:19.) That's a promise!

Thus, the key to consistently walking in the blessings of God is obedience. Obedience simply means doing what God says to do. Imagine a child constantly disregarding their parents' instructions and then being surprised and frustrated when they aren't rewarded for their behavior. God sometimes gives us gifts in spite of our disobedience. However, there is a very specific blessing that can be received only through obedience. God told the Israelites that if they would listen to His voice and do what was right in His sight, He would be their Great Physician. Obedience postures us to receive the full measure of God's favor.

What if a wealthy businessman told you he wanted to give you ten million dollars—the catch being that you would have to be at a particular local bank by nine o'clock the next morning? Now, imagine that you arrive at the bank at noon. What would happen? You would not receive the ten million dollars. You would have missed your opportunity to receive that blessing. Even though you went to the bank, you did not arrive at the right time. Many Christians want to obey God on their own terms, but that is not possible. If you will commit to being obedient to God's Word, I guarantee that you will begin to walk in the greatest level of blessings you have ever seen or experienced in your life.

Day 14: BREAKTHROUGH PRAYER

Father, You said in Your Word that if I am willing and obedient, I will eat the good of the land. I desire to walk in the fullness of Your blessings for my life. Therefore, I commit myself, by faith, to walking in a spirit of obedience. You said that we are to be *"doers of the word, and not hearers only."* Therefore, I declare that I am a doer of the Word of God and not a hearer of the Word only. It is my delight to do what is pleasing in Your sight. My heart's desire is to obey Your Word in everything. I declare that I am an obedient follower of Your precepts. Through the help of the Holy Spirit, I am faithful in the assignment You have given me, and I will not deviate from the path of obedience. I declare that my path is *"the path of the just,"* and it gets brighter and brighter *"to the perfect day."* In Jesus's name, amen. (See James 1:22; 1 John 3:22; Proverbs 4:18.)

Day 15: Who Do You Say That I Am?

[Jesus] *says to them, But whom say you that I am?*
(Matthew 16:15)

If there is one thing I have learned about God, it is that He always asks questions that He already knows the answers to. For example, after the fall, God asked Adam, "*Where are you?*" (Genesis 3:9). Now, we know that God is omniscient, so He was not asking for information. Therefore, the question is, *Why* did He ask that question to begin with?

God often asks us questions to get us to examine our own perspective. In the gospel of Mark, Jesus asked His disciples, "*Whom do men say that I the Son of man am?*" (Matthew 16:13). There must come a time in our lives when we truly recognize the identity of the One whom we serve. And as we gain the revelation of who Jesus is, we gain the revelation of who *we* are. To Jesus's question, Peter answered, "*You are the Christ, the Son of the living God*" (verse 16). This was not just information—it was revelation from the Father. Jesus was so moved by this revelation that He declared to Peter, "*Upon this rock I will build My church*" (verse 18).

The church of the Lord Jesus Christ was never meant to be built upon information; it was meant to be built upon revelation. Specifically, the church is built on identity. At the foundation of every crisis in today's society is a lack of identity. Our identity in Christ shapes everything about who we are and what we do. As believers, once we know who we are and to whom we belong, we possess the keys to fulfill our destinies.

Who is Jesus to you? Like many people in society, do you see Him as a religious symbol? A relic? Merely a good person who did nice things? Or do you have a revelation of Him as the Son of God and the Deliverer of all mankind? The way you see Him will determine the way you exercise your faith (or don't exercise it). For example, once you recognize that Jesus is the Healer, you will begin to confidently appropriate His healing power in your life. Today, I want to challenge you to open your spiritual eyes and gain a revelatory understanding of the Savior and Lover of your soul.

Day 15: BREAKTHROUGH PRAYER

Father, I thank You for being my God and my Redeemer. You sent Your Son Jesus as the ultimate sacrifice for my sin, and as a result of His obedience, I am a new creation. Open my spiritual eyes to the true identity of Jesus. Thank You for revealing to me who I really am in Him. I'm no longer a slave to sin, fear, or the past, but I have been renewed in the image of my Creator. I declare that my identity as a child of God has been solidified by faith. Today is a new day! In Jesus's name, amen. (See 2 Corinthians 5:17; Colossians 3:10.)

Day 16: Arrested Destiny

In whom also we have obtained an inheritance, being predestinated according to the purpose of Him who works all things after the counsel of His own will. (Ephesians 1:11)

I'm a frequent traveler—not only within the United States, but also overseas. In fact, I probably spend more time in the air than I do on the ground. Okay, that's an exaggeration! But the point is that I've had my share of experiencing international travel. I will never forget the time I traveled to England and realized upon arrival that my bags had not arrived with me. All of my suits and ties, as well as other very important items, were in one of my suitcases. Even though I had arrived at my destination, the things I needed while I was in England were still in America.

My bags had essentially been "arrested" and detained. Among the definitions of *arrest* are "to seize (someone) by legal authority and take them into custody," and "to stop or check (progress or a process)." The process of transporting my luggage to England had definitely been checked. It would take three days before my bags reached the UK. Even after they arrived, I had to go through a very frustrating and time-consuming process to retrieve them.

Similarly, many people have experienced the arresting of their destinies. The enemy of our souls is constantly seeking opportunities to waylay the purposes and assignments God has for our lives. The good news is that, similar to my bags, our lives have already been "tagged" for our destinations. The airlines use tagging to determine where people's bags and other belongings should go. You, my friend, are marked for spiritual purpose. And by the grace of God, you *will* arrive at your destination.

Day 16: BREAKTHROUGH PRAYER

Father, I recognize that You have predestined me to be conformed to the image of Jesus. My life has an "itinerary" that You established before the foundation of the world. I declare that I will arrive at my destination, and that I will arrive *on time*. I declare that everything You have purposed in my life—including relationships, connections, material resources, and opportunities—will be present and active in my life and destiny. I take authority over the spirit of arrested destiny, and I command the enemy's hold to be released from every area of my life. In the name of Jesus, amen! (See Romans 8:29.)

Day 17: What's in Your Hand?

And the L*ORD* *said to him, What is that in your hand? And he said, A rod.* (Exodus 4:2)

One of my favorite stories in the Bible is the exodus of the children of Israel from Egypt. I love the fact that God used an unlikely hero in this story. Moses was a man who had been raised in Pharaoh's house. He was acclimated to the culture of Egypt. The only problem was that Moses was living a lie. He was trapped in an identity crisis because he was actually a Hebrew, not an Egyptian, and the Hebrew people were being oppressed by the Egyptians. Out of his fear and insecurity, he committed a heinous crime—murder—causing him to flee from Egypt and run into the wilderness. He ended up settling in Midian, marrying, and becoming a shepherd. (See Exodus 2.)

Forty years later, God got Moses's attention by the miracle of the burning bush, and He called him to lead the children of Israel out of their captivity in Egypt. During this encounter, the Lord asked Moses a profound question: *"What is that in your hand?"* (Exodus 4:2). Why was this question so significant? Most people don't realize that God frequently uses something in our possession to manifest His supernatural power in our lives. There are other biblical examples of this. For instance, when the prophet Elisha participated in God's miraculous provision for a poor widow, he asked the woman, *"What have you in the house?"* (2 Kings 4:2). Before Jesus fed the five thousand, He asked the disciples, *"How many loaves have you?"* (Mark 6:38).

Thus, God often uses natural things to produce supernatural results. In other words, He wants to place His "super" on your natural. What has God already given you that, once yielded to Him, might become a catalyst for supernatural breakthrough? I challenge you to lift your hands to God today and say, "Father, have Your way; I am available to You."

Day 17: BREAKTHROUGH PRAYER

Father, in the name of Jesus, I thank You for who You are and all that You have done in my life. I declare that Your Word is mighty. I recognize that You desire to place Your "super" on my natural. Therefore, I am making available to You every resource in my possession. I give You permission to transform what's in my hand into a catalyst for supernatural breakthrough. I surrender my time, my talents, and my treasures to You. I release my faith for the manifestation of Your supernatural power in and through my life. In Jesus's name, amen.

Day 18: Elisha's Prayer

And Elisha prayed, and said, Lord, I pray You, open his eyes, that he may see. And the Lord opened the eyes of the young man; and he saw: and, behold, the mountain was full of horses and chariots of fire round about Elisha.

(2 Kings 6:17)

Gehazi, the servant of the prophet Elisha, woke up one morning and saw the city surrounded by horses and chariots. The king of Syria had sent soldiers to bring Elisha to him, because he'd found out the prophet had been revealing his secret plans to the king of Israel. Panicked, Gehazi asked Elisha, in effect, "What are we going to do?" Elisha responded, *"Fear not: for they that be with us are more than they that be with them."* (See 2 Kings 6:15–16.)

Have you ever felt like you were surrounded by enemies? Have you looked around and noticed that worry, fear, insecurity, or chaotic family issues seemed to be closing in on you on every side? Have you ever woken up and said to God in a panic, "Lord, what are we going to do? What are *You* going to do?" You may have felt that way last year, last month, or even just this morning. Many times, we tend to get carried away by what we see in the natural and completely disregard what is happening in the spiritual realm. But we can trust that God is active in our lives, no matter what the circumstances look like. The Lord Jesus says that the heavenly Father is always working. (See John 5:17 NIV.)

Elisha prayed that his servant's eyes would be opened to see the activity happening beyond his natural sight, and Gehazi immediately saw numerous fiery chariots and horses on the mountain. God had sent an army to support them! Accordingly, every time a problem arises, allow your spiritual eyes to see beyond your natural understanding. The solution to any problem is always available to us; we gain access to it through prayer and belief in the promises of God's Word. God has already supplied what you need for any present or future situation. Remember this, speak it, and thank Him for it! I declare to you the words Elisha spoke to his servant: "Do not fear—there are more with you than there are with them!" With God on your side, you are the majority! Beloved, don't you believe He will do the same for you as He did for Elisha if you will only ask? Believe and declare what God has spoken, and you will see that the armies of heaven are at your disposal, ready to do battle on your behalf!

Day 18: BREAKTHROUGH PRAYER

Father, Your Word tells me that You are always with me, and that if God is for me, who can be against me? Weapons may be formed against me, but they cannot prosper in my life, in Jesus's name! I do not fear, because You are on my side. You show me strategies and give me instructions to solve any problem. I trust You completely, and when enemies of my faith like worry, despair, fear, and confusion attempt to surround me, I look up and see Your provision and protection encircling me on every side. I declare that no enemy of my faith has power over me, because greater is He who lives within me than he who is in the world! I will keep my spiritual eyes open so that I don't miss a moment of the glorious things You are doing in my life and in the lives of those around me. You are the God who defends me; You are my Banner of Victory. I can't lose, because You are with me. In Jesus's name, amen! (See Psalm 139:7–10; Matthew 28:20; Romans 8:31; Isaiah 54:17; Psalm 118:6; John 4:4; Exodus 17:15–16 NIV.)

Day 19: The Accelerator

And Jesus put forth His hand, and touched him, saying, I will; be you clean. And immediately his leprosy was cleansed. (Matthew 8:3)

I remember first learning how to drive. The vehicle I learned with had manual transmission, also known as "stick shift." With manual transmission, the gear you are in determines how fast you can accelerate. This aspect was fascinating to me as a young person. As you place your foot on a pedal, you release gasoline into the pistons, and that causes the car to move faster. Of course, that pedal is call the "accelerator."

The word *accelerator* is defined as "a person or thing that causes something to happen or develop more quickly." As much as I like cars, the purpose of my description is not to discuss the mechanics of driving—I am illustrating a spiritual pattern for supernatural breakthrough. God's anointing is the "accelerator." In Matthew 8, the leprous man had been trapped in neutral as a result of his condition, but the anointing of the Holy Spirit through the hands of our Lord was more than enough to immediately accelerate him out of his situation, bringing him into a state of wholeness and new life.

God desires to accelerate you right now! He wants to move you out of neutral and into fifth gear. Your life is about to experience a shift like you have never dreamed or imagined. Release your faith right now for a change. It doesn't matter how long you've been trapped or stuck where you are—the glory of the

Lord is about to move you into a new dimension. Healing and wholeness are your portion!

Day 19: BREAKTHROUGH PRAYER

Father, I thank You for the anointing of the Holy Spirit. Lord Jesus, I recognize that You are more than able to accelerate me into my God-given destiny and cause me to fulfill the purpose that You have ordained for my life. I refuse to be stuck in the same gear; I choose to move forward. I surrender my life and my will to You, and I ask You to transform me and move me into the plans that You have for my life and for my family. I declare that I am moving forward and upward in the name of Jesus. I declare that my life is about to look much different than it does right now. I declare that healing and wholeness are my portion. In Jesus's name, amen.

Day 20: Understanding Your Purpose

In whom also we have obtained an inheritance, being predestinated according to the purpose of Him who works all things after the counsel of His own will. (Ephesians 1:11)

Purpose is defined as "the reason for which something is done or created or for which something exists." Everything God created has a purpose, and therefore God has a purpose for each of us. As the Lord said to the prophet Jeremiah, *"Before I formed you in the belly I knew you; and before you came forth out of the womb I sanctified you, and I ordained you a prophet to the nations"* (Jeremiah 1:5).

The late Dr. Myles Munroe used to say, "Where purpose is unknown, abuse is inevitable." Nothing could ring more true! Purpose is like jet fuel—no matter how big or beautiful a plane may be, without fuel, it cannot take off into the air. Purpose is power! The enemy of your soul doesn't want you to take flight into your destiny, and so he has consistently attempted to ground you. But I declare to you today that the devil is a liar and a usurper. Today is the day when you will begin to release your miraculous potential. Where purpose is known and acted upon, success is inevitable.

You must decide now to be a person of purpose. There is a specific reason for your existence, and once you discover that reason, your life will be transformed. The catch is this: God has not called you to pursue purpose; He has called you to pursue a Person—Himself. Yet the more you get to know the Father intimately, the more you will discover the purpose He has for your life. God is looking for a generation of people who understand their purpose and identity—and act accordingly.

Day 20: BREAKTHROUGH PRAYER

> Father, I recognize that You are a God of purpose, and I acknowledge that You have a good plan for my life. Your Word declares that You know the plans You have for me. I declare that I am a person of purpose; therefore, I am certain to experience success and prosperity. I declare that the enemy's plans for my life have failed. I declare that I am moving upward and onward according to Your perfect design for my life. I declare that my life will never be the same from this day forward and that I will experience unusual success and favor. In the name of Jesus, amen. (See Jeremiah 29:11 NIV, AMP.)

Day 21: Faith Is...

Now faith is the substance of things hoped for, the evidence of things not seen. (Hebrews 11:1)

There is nothing more vital to the Christian experience than faith. Many people would cite prayer, intimacy with God, or love as being supreme—but each of these is connected to our faith in God. The Bible says, "*He that comes to God must believe that He is, and that He is a rewarder of them that diligently seek Him*" (Hebrews 11:6). The foundation of our faith is the confidence that God is who He says He is. The more we operate in the revealed knowledge of God, the more we will experience breakthrough and victory in our lives.

You may be experiencing a difficulty in your life right now. Let me reassure you that God is the Deliverer. God is the Provider. God is the Healer. Yet faith sees the nature and character of God, not just the ability of God. We must make a decision not to be manipulated or persuaded by our circumstances, but rather be fully persuaded by our faith in God and His Word. The term "*substance*" in Hebrews 11 comes from the Greek word *hypostasis,* which literally means "a setting under," or "support." In other words, faith is a support system for every area of our spiritual lives. Without faith, we cannot please God! (See Hebrews 11:6.) But through faith, not only are we able to please God, but we are also able to confidently receive the things He has freely given to us. So beloved, do not be moved by what you see, but stand on the Word of God. Whatever

He has promised, He is faithful to perform. (See, for example, Hebrews 10:23.) Faith is the revelation of God's Word in action; therefore, believe His Word and confidently act upon what He has spoken.

Day 21: BREAKTHROUGH PRAYER

Father, Your Word is true! *"Faith is the substance of things hoped for, the evidence of things not seen"*; therefore, I declare that I possess unwavering faith in Your Word. My faith is the evidence that convicts my conscience and serves as the proof that what You have spoken, You are able to perform. I am not moved by my circumstances, but I am confident in Your eternal Word. I wait with great anticipation to see and experience the manifestation of Your glorious promises. My faith allows me to access the realm of the invisible and receive supernatural blessings in every area of my life. I possess my healing and my deliverance by faith. Nothing is impossible to me because I am a believer in Your Word and not a doubter. By faith, I release supernatural breakthrough in my life. Thank You in advance for the manifestation of what You have promised. In Jesus's name, amen!

Day 22: Make Room for Your Miracle

And she [the Shunammite woman] *said to her husband, Behold now, I perceive that this is a holy man of God, which passes by us continually. Let us make a little chamber, I pray you, on the wall; and let us set for him there a bed, and a table, and a stool, and a candlestick: and it shall be, when he comes to us, that he shall turn in there.*

(2 Kings 4:9–10)

Are you prepared for what God desires to do in your life? I know that might seem like a strange question, but it is a very important one. In other words, can you accommodate what you are praying for?

I will never forget the first time I bought a car on my own. I was in college, and I was so excited about that vehicle—it was a good car, it was exactly the color I wanted, and it was fast. However, I didn't have a lot of experience taking care of cars. Once, when I took the vehicle to be serviced, the technician asked me when I had last taken it for an oil change. I told him it had been a year. He started to laugh hysterically!

The truth was, I wasn't ready to own a car of that caliber. Similarly, many Christians all over the world are asking God for things they don't have the capacity to receive. What will you do after you receive what you have prayed for? Are you prepared for that spouse? Are you ready for that promotion? Have you developed the life of prayer and devotion necessary to sustain your dream ministry or next assignment?

It is clear that one of the keys to supernatural breakthrough is preparation. The Shunammite woman recognized that Elisha was a man of God, so she extended special hospitality to him. By creating space for the prophet, she was actually making room for a miracle. We must take notes from the life of this great woman of faith and get into position ourselves to receive the things we are believing God for. The Shunammite woman had no idea she would become a mother after years of barrenness, simply by being wise enough to make room for one who was doing God's work. But she opened her life to God's blessings. (See 2 Kings 4:14–17.)

Change your thinking! Change your attitude! Take on a different disposition. Remember, the attitude of expectancy is the breeding ground for miracles. Don't wait until you see the manifestation. Make room now!

Day 22: BREAKTHROUGH PRAYER

Father, You are the Lord of the breakthrough, and I know that You have met every need in my life. By faith, I receive Your miraculous provision and all the blessings You have graciously prepared for Your children. I position myself to receive the manifestation of Your promises in my life. I declare that my thoughts, words, and actions will align with heaven's agenda. I recognize that now is the time of my supernatural visitation. In Jesus's name, amen!

Day 23: What Do You See?

> *Moreover the word of the* LORD *came to me, saying, Jeremiah, what see you? And I said, I see a rod of an almond tree.* (Jeremiah 1:11)

I vividly remember watching crime movies as a kid. I specifically recall scenes in which a character would sit down in front of a psychologist, who would hold up inkblots and ask the person to describe what they saw. These were abstract images whose interpretation was up to the viewer. However, the analysis of what they saw in those images revealed the type of personality they had.

Likewise, God has "tests" He uses to help us understand ourselves. In an earlier devotional, I talked about how God often asks us questions He already knows the answers to. Throughout the Scriptures, we can see a tapestry of God causing people to examine themselves and their way of viewing their situations. In the same way, He wants *you* to recognize the way you view the world because your perspective determines your potential. Change a faulty perspective, and you unlock latent potential!

One of the most important skills you and I can learn is how to open our spiritual eyes to see things from heaven's perspective. When we see what heaven sees and know what heaven possesses, we will begin to reflect that vision and knowledge. Are you looking at life through defeated lenses? Are you wearing the bifocals of fear? The Bible says that we should be transformed by the renewing of our minds. (See Romans 12:2.) Once you change your thinking, you will change your perspective. Once you change your perspective, you will unlock your potential. Make a decision today to look at the world through the lens of heaven.

Day 23: BREAKTHROUGH PRAYER

Father, in the name of Jesus, I declare that Your power is presently manifesting in my life. I choose today to look at the world through the lens of heaven. I refuse and refute any form of victimhood or oppression in my life. I recognize that You are very interested in my perspective, because perspective determines potential. I declare that I have unlimited potential in You. My life will never be stagnant, broken, barren, or frustrated, in the name of Jesus. All spiritual blindness is removed from my life. I declare that my spiritual eyes are open and I am able to see You clearly. Your Word says that as we behold You in Your glory, we are changed into Your image "*from glory to glory*"; therefore, I declare that as I look on You with spiritual eyes, I am conformed to Your image. Thank You, Lord, for radically reshaping and transforming my life. In Jesus's name, amen. (See 2 Corinthians 3:18.)

Day 24: No Limits, No Boundaries

And Jabez called on the God of Israel, saying, Oh that You would bless me indeed, and enlarge my coast, and that Your hand might be with me, and that You would keep me from evil, that it may not grieve me! And God granted him that which he requested. (1 Chronicles 4:10)

Another of my favorite stories in the Bible is the account of Jabez. The Scripture records that Jabez was more honorable than his brothers. Ironically, the name *Jabez* means "sorrow." (See 1 Chronicles 4:9.) Yet Jabez prayed one of the boldest prayers in the Bible. He asked God if He would bless him and enlarge his "*coast*," or "*territory*" (NIV).

Many times, we seem to experience limitations or setbacks in our lives. Whether these limits are real or imagined, the effect is the same: not reaching the destiny God has for us. I believe that each one of us can learn from the prayer of Jabez. We must be bold enough to insist on a life without limitation. Maybe you're going through a terrible divorce. Maybe someone has walked away from you. Maybe you have received a negative medical diagnosis. No matter where you are in life, God desires to bless you and enlarge your territory. It is time to move beyond limitation and experience supernatural breakthrough.

Do not allow any situation to limit you from becoming everything you were intended to be. Your enemies are about to be confounded by the marvelous manifestation of God's favor in your life. The Holy Spirit desires to reveal the heart of the

Father to you today. I want you to know that God never intended for you to remain in your brokenness. He never intended for that sickness or disease to overcome you. You are about to break through and stretch forth into supernatural abundance. Do not let your circumstances define you; let your faith in God's Word be the defining reality that governs your life. Hallelujah!

Day 24: BREAKTHROUGH PRAYER

Father, in the name of Jesus, I thank You for the power of the Holy Spirit. I know beyond a shadow of a doubt that Jesus Christ rose from the dead. Therefore, I declare that no prison of fear, discouragement, hurt, disappointment, depression, oppression, rejection, addiction, poverty, or illness has the power to hold me in captivity. I declare that I live a life without limits. I exercise my faith right now to receive the abundance You have graciously designed for me. I refuse to live in lack. I refuse to be bound by sin or iniquity. I receive a heavenly quality of life. Thank You, Father, for blessing me indeed, and for enlarging my territory, causing me to triumph over my enemies. In Jesus's name, amen!

Day 25: The Unseen Realm

Through faith we understand that the worlds were framed by the word of God, so that things which are seen were not made of things which do appear. (Hebrews 11:3)

Years ago, I heard a story about several young students who participated in a science project. Their teacher had brought them to a lake, where they were asked to take samples of the water. The instructor then asked the students what they saw in the water they had collected. They didn't see anything, because the water was fairly clear. Then they took the water to the school lab, put some of it on a petri dish, and placed it under a microscope. As the students looked in the microscope, to their surprise, they saw that the water was teeming with life. Even though the organisms in the water were unseen to the naked eye, they were very much real. Over the years, numerous biology students worldwide have had a similar experience.

People often think that "unseen" equates to being "unreal," but nothing could be further from the truth. The unseen realm, or spiritual realm, is just as real—if not more real—than our natural world. How many times have you used a cellular phone? Now, how many times have you seen a cellular frequency? We never question the reality and power of our cellular devices, even though we can't see how they operate. Yet millions of people do not know about or acknowledge the spiritual world—with many people denying its existence and reality.

Today, God desires to open your spiritual eyes so you can see the supernatural realities around you. Faith is the microscope—and telescope—of the spiritual realm. That is why the Bible says, "*Through faith we understand that the worlds were framed by the word of God, so that things which are seen were not made of things which do appear.*" How would our lives change if we really understood this spiritual truth? God's words created the physical world; in the same way, God's words will change your world. Speak the Word of God and watch the unseen come into manifestation.

Day 25: BREAKTHROUGH PRAYER

Father, I recognize that You are here in the "eternal now," and I also acknowledge that the invisible realm is more real and tangible than the visible realm. Open my spiritual eyes to perceive and understand the supernatural realities of Your kingdom. I declare that my spiritual eyes are open to see angels. I declare that my spiritual ears are receptive to heavenly wisdom. I declare that I am able to recognize Your supernatural solutions. Father, grant me heavenly vision. I declare that I look beyond my circumstances as I hold on to the reality of Your Word. In Jesus's name, amen.

Day 26: The "Breaker" Anointing

> *The breaker is come up before them: they have broken up, and have passed through the gate, and are gone out by it: and their king shall pass before them, and the* Lord *on the head of them.* (Micah 2:13)

When I was growing up, I watched a lot of martial arts movies on television, and I would often try to imitate the moves I saw the characters perform. On one such occasion, I was trying to demonstrate a particular move. I stood in front of a mirror because I wanted to see myself do this special kick. As you can probably imagine, the situation didn't end well. The result: shattered glass all over the floor—and several stitches in my leg. As bad as the story might sound, it reminds me of many people in the body of Christ today. There are millions of believers who need the "glass ceiling" that is restricting them to be shattered so they can go on to the next level of growth and prosperity—millions who need a supernatural breakthrough in their lives.

The Bible tells us that it is the anointing that actually destroys the yoke. (See Isaiah 10:27.) Note that it doesn't just break the yoke—it destroys it! This means that the yoke cannot be reassembled. Whatever has held you in captivity is about to be destroyed right now. The good news is that the "breaker" anointing, a term taken from Micah 2:13, is in you by virtue of the presence of the Holy Spirit. But you must release this anointing by placing a demand on it by faith.

There was a time in my life in which my ministry did not seem to be making any headway. Finally, God gave me a revelation of the necessity and power of the breaker anointing to release stagnation and delay. Once I tapped into this supernatural power by faith, things began to change. Today, through the breaker anointing, things are going to change for you, too!

Day 26: BREAKTHROUGH PRAYER

Father, thank You for the breaker anointing. Today, I declare that this anointing will manifest in my life and in the lives of my loved ones. Every hindrance, setback, limitation, or stagnation I am experiencing in my life is removed today, in Jesus's name. Longstanding addictions and life-controlling issues are broken by the power of the Holy Spirit right now. Doors are opened, chains are broken, and limits are lifted. No weapon formed against me will be able to prosper. I declare that all sickness and disease is removed right now. I take authority over every spirit of delay in my life and in the lives of those for whom I am praying, and I declare that supernatural acceleration is our portion. Our lives are filled with the fullness of God. In Jesus's name, amen. (See Isaiah 54:17; Ephesians 3:19.)

Day 27: When *Chronos* Meets *Kairos*

Jesus says to him, Rise, take up your bed, and walk.
(John 5:8)

The biblical account of the lame man at the Pool of Bethesda illustrates many spiritual truths. (See John 5:1–9.) I have actually had the opportunity to visit the ruins of this ancient pool in Israel, which could accommodate thousands of people in its day. This man had been afflicted for thirty-eight years, and he had waited by the pool for a very long time to receive a miracle from God. Unfortunately, he was never able to realize his dream of getting into the pool at the right time in order to obtain his healing.

As this man was lying by the pool, Jesus came along and invited him into a most unlikely place—a placed called "now." You see, this man's problem was not his infirm state; his greatest enemy was time. The New Testament generally has two words for "time." The first is *chronos,* which means chronological time. The second is *kairos,* which means "opportune" time, or a divine moment when God suspends, overrides, or interrupts the natural timeline. The lame man at the pool was trapped in a prison of *chronos* time—the years stretching from the past into the present in which he had been bedridden, and apparently always would be. However, the Lord Jesus set him free and empowered him to experience *kairos* time. God lives in the eternal *now,* and that's exactly where miracles reside. Jesus told this man to rise, take up his bed, and walk. And he did! This was not a gradual or natural healing. This was an instant, miraculous manifestation of *kairos*. When eternity invades time, miracles happen. God is calling you to rise, take up your bed, and walk right now. Do you believe?

Day 27: BREAKTHROUGH PRAYER

Father, in the name of Jesus, I thank You for the power of the Holy Spirit. I know that You are the God of all eternity. You are here in the eternal now. Right now, I release my faith so that eternity will invade time and bring into manifestation everything that You have promised me. I refuse to be bound or stuck in my current situation. Instead, I release my faith to receive Your greater, eternal reality. I am ready to make use of every opportunity You have afforded me. Lord Jesus, thank You for setting me free from bondage to time and enabling me to rise above the natural order of things. I know that You are moving right now on my behalf. In Jesus's name, amen.

Day 28: Will You Be Made Whole?

When Jesus saw him lie, and knew that he had been now a long time in that case, He says to him, Will you be made whole? (John 5:6)

One of the simplest—but most powerful—realities of the New Testament is that God wants us to be whole. What is wholeness? Wholeness means that nothing is missing and nothing is broken. God wants us to be fully furnished and thoroughly supplied. The man at the Pool of Bethesda, whom we discussed in yesterday's devotional, had a serious problem: he was disconnected from God. His sin and his sickness had alienated him from God's perfect will. As a result, he was waiting for the "*water*" (John 5:7) to move so he could be healed—since an angel would supposedly stir the water and allow those who could make it into the water in time to be made well.

Are you waiting for the "water" to move? That is, are you waiting for God to do something that He has actually already done? Ironically, the lame man was waiting for God to move—but God was waiting for him to move. "*Rise, take up your bed, and walk*" (John 5:8) were Jesus's timeless words to the man. The Greek word translated "*rise*" means "to waken," or "to rouse"—as when you wake someone up who is sleeping. This man was in a "slumbering" state—both spiritually and physically. The next thing Jesus told the man to do was to take up his bed. This phrase refers to an exercise of the will—to deliberately decide to no longer be in the situation that one is in. Notice that Jesus didn't take up the bed for him. The man had to take up his own bed. Lastly, Jesus told him to *"walk."* The original Greek term means, among other things, "to make due use of opportunities."

What opportunity have you missed as a result of your bondage? It is time for you to make a decision that you are no longer going to be bedridden, but you are going to be bound to your God-given destiny. Wholeness is your portion, because Jesus has provided an abundant life for us. Will you receive it?

Day 28: BREAKTHROUGH PRAYER

Father, in the matchless name of Jesus, I hear Your voice today. Your Word declares that "Your sheep hear Your voice, and a stranger they will not follow." I realize that You are inviting me to experience Your abundant life. I refuse to camp by the pool of despair. I refuse to dwell in a ditch of depression. Lord Jesus, You are the living Word, and Your Word is powerful and miraculous. I respond to Your invitation to receive supernatural life. Your Word tells me to *"arise"* and *"shine."* Nothing will keep me from arising and shining. I will no longer rest upon any affliction, pain, sickness, or rejection. I will walk out my destiny with faith and confidence in You. Today is an awesome day because I serve an awesome God! In Jesus's name, amen. (See John 10:1–5; Isaiah 60:1.)

Day 29: Wake Up!

And that, knowing the time, that now it is high time to awake out of sleep: for now is our salvation nearer than when we believed. (Romans 13:11)

I grew up in Georgia, and one of my most vivid memories is of going to school early in the morning. In the wintertime, it could get quite cold, but we still had to go out and wait for the bus in order to go to school. I remember my father frequently having to yell, "Wake up! Wake up!" I wouldn't move from my bed until the inevitable happened—he would snatch the blanket off me, and my body would be exposed to that Georgia cold. That would get me up!

I look back and laugh at the situation. But, in a similar way, God is a good Father to us, calling out, "Wake up, wake up, wake up!" He wants us to be in a spiritual state of full consciousness. Many people are physically awake but spiritually asleep. In essence, they are sleepwalking. They don't know their purpose, their assignment, or their destiny. As a result of their spiritual slumber, they spend their lives in frustration. That is not God's perfect will for you. He wants you to be fully awake and aware of what He is speaking to you and what He is doing in your life. Most human beings will spend the majority of their lives "sleeping," but God has a better spiritual plan. He wants us to seek Him with all our hearts. Wake up early to pray and start your day with fervency and zeal. I declare that you have come out of darkness and are walking in the marvelous light of Jesus Christ! (See Isaiah 9:2; 2 Corinthians 4:6.)

Day 29: BREAKTHROUGH PRAYER

Father, in the name of Jesus, I thank You for who You are and all that You have done in my life. Today, I will arise and shine and operate from the heavenly realm! Your light has come, and Your glory has risen upon me. I rise up from spiritual slumber and complacency, in the name of Jesus. My spiritual eyes and ears are open to You. I hear You clearly and do the things that are pleasing in Your sight. I am sensitive to Your presence and I am led by Your Spirit. Thank You for opening the eyes of my understanding and enlightening my heart to be receptive to Your divine wisdom. In Jesus's name, amen. (See Isaiah 60:1–2; 1 John 3:22.)

Day 30: Much More than Crumbs

And she said, Truth, Lord: yet the dogs eat of the crumbs which fall from their masters' table. (Matthew 15:27)

There is a woman who will probably go down in history as simultaneously being the most enigmatic and the most audacious woman in the Bible. (See Matthew 15:21–28.) When she encountered Jesus, she was in dire circumstances. *"And, behold, a woman of Canaan came out of the same coasts, and cried to Him, saying, Have mercy on me, O Lord, [O] Son of David; my daughter is grievously vexed with a devil"* (verse 22). This woman's daughter was being tormented, and like any good parent, she was willing to do whatever it took to see her child set free. Apparently, amid the racial and cultural tensions of the day, Jesus's disciples didn't see things that way—they asked that she be sent away. Syro-Phoenicians, Samaritans, and Canaanites were generally despised by the Jews at that time, and in the prejudicial viewpoint of the disciples, she was no different from all the rest of the "undesirables."

Yet Jesus was up to something. As the woman persisted, He said, *"I am not sent but to the lost sheep of the house of Israel"* (verse 24). However, in her audacity and need, she continued to worship Him. Finally, Jesus told her plainly, *"It is not meet to take the children's bread, and to cast it to dogs"* (verse 26). You would think she would be hurt, offended, and frustrated, but her response is shocking: *"And she said, Truth, Lord: yet the dogs eat of the crumbs which fall from their masters' table."* Wow! In her faith and desperation, she was willing to be embarrassed, humiliated, and rejected if it meant receiving the "crumbs" of healing for her daughter. In that moment, she broke through. She moved from desperation to expectation and finally manifestation when Jesus said, *"O woman, great is your faith: be it to you even as you will"* (verse 28). Her daughter was delivered! She was willing to receive crumbs, and she received so much more. I believe Jesus was actually saying to this woman, "I don't want you to settle for crumbs; I am inviting you to the table." He was getting her to recognize that she was not a dog but a treasured daughter of the Most High God. Many times, we face challenges, and in our desperation, we settle for whatever we can get, when, in fact, the Father desires to lavish His abundant grace upon our lives. Are you willing to *press in* to receive the greater blessing? God prepares a table before you today! (See Psalm 23:5.) Receive!

Day 30: BREAKTHROUGH PRAYER

Father, Your Word speaks of the righteous never being forsaken, and their seed never begging for bread. I recognize that Jesus is the Bread of Life. He gave Himself as a ransom to save us. I declare that Your provisions of healing and deliverance are mine, in the name of Jesus. Right now, I receive total deliverance and healing on behalf of my loved ones, friends, neighbors, and coworkers. I release my faith in Your supernatural power. Lord, You are benevolent and gracious; therefore, I posture myself to receive all that You have provided for me. I will not settle for crumbs. I receive *more*. In Jesus's name, amen! (See Psalm 37:25; John 6:35, 51; Matthew 20:28.)

Day 31: The Power of Expectancy

> [Abraham] *against hope believed in hope, that he might become the father of many nations; according to that which was spoken, So shall your seed be.* (Romans 4:18)

There is something about hope that moves the hand of God. The Bible actually says, "*We are saved by hope*" (Romans 8:24). The word "*hope*" here means confident expectation of good. The attitude of expectancy is the atmosphere for miracles. "*Faith is the substance of things hoped for*" (Hebrews 11:1). In other words, our faith is what gives substance to our expectation.

What are you expecting today? What are you anticipating that God will do? One of the biggest enemies of expectancy is discouragement. When we are discouraged, we don't look forward to good things happening. Every morning on our church's international prayer call, I say, "Something good is going to happen to you!" Why? Because I believe it with all my heart, and you should too. Every day, when I wake up, I look forward to God doing something miraculous in my life that day.

Scripture says that we should enter the kingdom of God like children. (See, for example, Matthew 18:3.) Children are creatures of expectancy. If you tell them they are going to have ice cream after school, they will shout with excitement and anticipation long before they see or taste a single scoop. This is how we ought to be as children of God. We should be expectant of miracles at every turn. How would your life change if you began to take on that attitude daily?

I believe that something good is going to happen to you today! Release your faith for more! We serve a miracle-working God. You will experience what you expect.

Day 31: BREAKTHROUGH PRAYER

Father, Your Word declares that *"we are saved by hope."* Therefore, I confidently expect and await with great anticipation the blessings that You have graciously prepared for me. I am excited about the supernatural favor You have placed upon my life. Doors swing open for me! People of influence favor me because of Your mighty hand. Destiny-helpers are available to assist in the assignment You have for me. This is the day You have made, and I will rejoice and be glad in it! My life will never be the same again. In Jesus's name, amen! (See Psalm 118:24.)

Day 32: The Great Exchange

But the hour comes, and now is, when the true worshippers shall worship the Father in spirit and in truth: for the Father seeks such to worship him. (John 4:23)

It has been said that we were created to worship God. I believe this is true, but what does it really mean? The Scriptures teach us that God desires intimate fellowship with us. This truth may fly in the face of certain religious jargon that suggests we are just useless piles of clay. I believe the exact opposite is true. We are valuable—because our Creator is valuable and loves us deeply. As the old folks where I come from say, "God don't make no mess."

But what is worship? Worship is simply pouring out our adoration and devotion on the One who made us. We praise God for what He has done, but we worship Him for who He is. True worship is not a religious activity; it is a lifestyle fueled by revelation. Jesus told the woman at the well, *"God is a Spirit: and they that worship Him must worship Him in spirit and in truth"* (John 4:24). Jesus's statement tells us that worship is a function of our spirit and not our emotions. Please don't misunderstand what I am saying here. Worship can evoke great emotion, but the essence of our worship is not emotion.

Worship is the great exchange. As we worship the Father *"in spirit,"* He exchanges things with us: We give Him our "ashes," and He gives us His beauty. We give Him our heavy hearts, and He gives us the "garment of praise." (See Isaiah 61:3.) Worship is the only activity that allows us to experience the atmosphere of heaven while we are on the earth. The more we worship, the more heaven's reality manifests in our lives. I challenge you to create a habit of sincere worship. Worship doesn't have to take place only in your local church; it can take place in your living room, in your car, or elsewhere. But wherever it takes place, it must be done by the Spirit. Then you will begin to reap the true rewards of worship.

Day 32: BREAKTHROUGH PRAYER

Father, in the name of Jesus, I recognize that You created me to worship You. I was made in Your image and according to Your likeness. It is my deepest desire to connect with You in intimate fellowship. Father, I recognize that You have ordained a lifestyle of worship for every born-again believer. I worship You for who You are, not just for what You have done in my life. Worship is based upon revelation; therefore, as I worship You "*in spirit and in truth,*" I release wells of supernatural wisdom. I devote myself to You and reaffirm my faith in Your supernatural power. I declare that worship is my lifestyle every single day. In Jesus's name, amen.

Day 33: Resurrection Power

> *But if the Spirit of Him that raised up Jesus from the dead dwell in you, He that raised up Christ from the dead shall also quicken your mortal bodies by His Spirit that dwells in you.* (Romans 8:11)

The Scripture tells us that the same Spirit who raised Jesus from the dead dwells within us. If you really embraced that truth, how would it change the way you view your life right now? I often hear people make the statement, "I'm only human." This is a socially acceptable statement—but it is not a biblical one. You are not just human. As a born-again believer, you have the same Spirit who resurrected our Lord dwelling within you! The God of all creation lives inside you. The more conscious you are of the Risen One living within you, the more you are able to release His power in your life.

The Holy Spirit is much more than a religious phenomenon—He is a living Person; He is the very Spirit of God and of Jesus Christ. If you could really comprehend who dwells within you, you would never accept a mediocre existence again. I challenge you to change the way you look at yourself. I challenge you to refuse to live in a defeated way. I challenge you to recognize that there is power inside you.

One of the Greek words translated "power" in the New Testament is *dunamis,* which refers to miracle-working power. It is where we get the English word *dynamite*. So, the next time someone asks you how you're doing, I want you to tell them,

"I'm dynamite!" The dynamic power of heaven is working on your behalf. All you have to do is believe and release your faith for the miraculous power of God to operate in every area of your life.

Day 33: BREAKTHROUGH PRAYER

Father, in the name of Jesus, I thank You for changing me. I thank You for the life-giving power of restoration that lives inside me. The fullness of the Spirit of Christ lives within me, and I am working in partnership with the dynamic power of heaven. I declare that God's miracle-working power is touching and transforming every area of my life. I no longer walk in defeat but according to the dynamic power of God. I am victorious, in Jesus's name. Amen.

Day 34: Radical Obedience

Obey My voice, and I will be your God, and you shall be My people: and walk you in all the ways that I have commanded you, that it may be well to you. (Jeremiah 7:23)

When I was growing up, my siblings and I would often get in trouble for not following all of our parents' instructions. For example, if I was asked to do two things, but I did only one of them, that was grounds for disciplinary action. Why? Because I did not obey everything I was told to do.

God wants us to walk in *"all the ways"* that He has commanded us. I remember a particular instance when my wife and I were in church on a Sunday morning. A voice came to me and told me to empty out my pockets and give the money to someone who was in need. At first, I thought the suggestion had come from the enemy. But I quickly realized that the voice speaking to me was not Satan, but God. I did exactly what the Lord told me to do, and a blessing immediately followed.

Many Christians do not understand the concept of radical obedience. Radical obedience simply means doing exactly what God tells you to do, when He tells you to do it. I am sorry to inform you that delayed obedience is still disobedience. Every time God instructs us to do something, it's so that He can give us a blessing we are not currently experiencing. When God tells you to pray for someone, it's so that He can bless you as well as that other person. When God tells you to give, it's so that He can bless you, too. When God tells you to forgive, it's so that He can extend grace to you, as well.

Regardless of the situation, obedience is the key to the accelerated manifestation of God's blessings and favor in our lives. Remember that the Bible says, *"If you be willing and obedient, you shall eat the good of the land"* (Isaiah 1:19). Notice that willingness precedes obedience. Today, if you will make up in your mind that you are going to obey God—no matter the cost or the inconvenience—I believe your life will experience a supernatural shift.

Day 34: BREAKTHROUGH PRAYER

Father, in the name of Jesus, I thank You for who You are and all that You have done in my life. I declare that I walk in perfect obedience to Your will. I am willing and obedient; therefore, I will eat the good of the land all the days of my life. I am a doer of the Word and not just a hearer only. I delight myself in Your Word daily. As I meditate on Your Word with a desire to obey, I position myself for supernatural breakthrough. "Your sheep hear Your voice, and a stranger they do not follow." Therefore, I declare that I hear Your voice and am never led away by the voice of strangers. It is my delight to do that which is pleasing in Your sight. In Jesus's name, amen! (See James 1:22; Psalm 1:2; Psalm 119:16; John 10:1–5; 1 John 3:22.)

Day 35: Radical Breakthrough

And it came to pass, when she travailed, that the one put out his hand: and the midwife took and bound upon his hand a scarlet thread, saying, This came out first. And it came to pass, as he drew back his hand, that, behold, his brother came out: and she said, How have you broken forth? this breach be upon you: therefore his name was called Pharez. (Genesis 38:28–29)

I will never forget the day my son Isaac was born. As we were waiting for him to come forth, to our surprise, he literally burst out of the womb. In fact, he came so fast that if it weren't for the nurse who caught him by the heels, he would have literally hit the floor. It's appropriate that his name is Isaac, because every time we think about the story, we bust out in laughter.

In the above passage, the midwife who delivered Pharez experienced a similar situation. This baby's brother was set to come out of the womb first. Yet God had other plans, and Pharez became the firstborn. The name *Pharez* essentially means "breakthrough." Two characteristics of breakthrough are *sudden* and *supernatural*. Breakthroughs are not based on our level of education, affluence, or even natural talent; they are the result of the supernatural power of God.

I believe we are living in a season of supernatural breakthrough. In fact, you are about to embark on the greatest time of your life. The midwife asked Pharez, in effect, "How did you break through?" and people are going to ask you the same question when they see the supernatural manifestation of God's promises in your life. They will want to know: "How did your marriage turn around so quickly?" "How were you instantly healed?" "How did your ministry take off?"

My desire is to set you up for a radical breakthrough. And while breakthroughs are sudden, they are far from spontaneous—the key is faith. Don't forget that "*faith is the substance of things hoped for, the evidence of things not seen*" (Hebrews 11:1). Simply believe, and God will confirm His Word to you with signs and wonders. (See Mark 16:20.)

Day 35: BREAKTHROUGH PRAYER

Father, I acknowledge that You are the Lord of the breakthrough. I recognize that Your miraculous hand is in manifestation in my life. Supernatural doors open for me because I am connected to a supernatural God. I declare that I am in a season of release. Today, I will encounter miracles. I will experience the supernatural grace of God. I will testify of the goodness of the Lord in every area of my life. Many will ask me, "How did you break through?" I will answer them by declaring that miracles are my portion. In the mighty name of Jesus, amen.

Day 36: How Many Vessels Did You Borrow?

Then he said, Go, borrow you vessels abroad of all your neighbors, even empty vessels; borrow not a few.

(2 Kings 4:3)

One of the most fascinating stories in the Bible is found in chapter four of the book of 2 Kings. A widow found herself in a very difficult financial situation, being in tremendous debt. In that time and culture, when people got into serious debt, they or their family members faced the risk of indentured servitude, and this widow's two sons were, in effect, about to become slaves. As any mother would be, this precious woman was in distress, and she cried out to Elisha, the prophet of God.

Elisha asked her a very peculiar question: "What do you have in your house?" Why is this question so relevant? Remember, God often uses what is already in our possession as a basis for releasing breakthrough in our lives. The woman replied, "I don't have anything except a pot of oil." (See verse 2.) Notice that her statement is a contradiction. She said she didn't have anything, yet she possessed one pot of oil—and that oil was all she needed to receive her miracle. The prophet told her to go and borrow as many vessels as she possibly could and then to pour the oil into the vessels. She did exactly that, and the oil continued to flow until all the vessels she had gathered were full. When she told Elisha, he instructed her to sell the oil, pay all her debts, and live on the excess. (See verses 3–7.)

This incident speaks to three spiritual principles: the "law of the seed," radical obedience, and capacity. Often, when you ask God for a miracle, He will ask you for a seed. The degree to which this woman could receive a miracle was contingent upon the degree of her obedience. We are frequently interested in a miracle, but God is interested in increasing our spiritual capacity. In the case of the widow, the more vessels, the more the oil flowed. What's in your house today? As I expressed previously, what do you possess that, once yielded to God, can create a supernatural flow of favor and blessing? Offer it, and get ready to receive!

Day 36: BREAKTHROUGH PRAYER

Father, thank You for the power of Your Word. I recognize that one word from You can transform my life. I declare that I walk in radical obedience. My heart and mind are receptive to divine instructions. Whatever You tell me to do, I will do. I make my resources available to You. I declare that my time, talents, and strengths are at your disposal; do with them as You will. Lord, I'm ready to receive my miracle. Thank You for taking care of all my debt—spiritual and financial—by Your supernatural grace. In Jesus's name, amen! (See Matthew 8:5–8.)

Day 37: The Living Word

> *For the word of God is living and active and full of power [making it operative, energizing, and effective]. It is sharper than any two-edged sword, penetrating as far as the division of the soul and spirit [the completeness of a person], and of both joints and marrow [the deepest parts of our nature], exposing and judging the very thoughts and intentions of the heart.* (Hebrews 4:12 AMP)

The Bible says that *"in the beginning was the Word, and the Word was with God, and the Word was God"* (John 1:1). There is no doubt theologically that the Word of God is a Person—Jesus Christ—and not just a concept: *"And the Word was made flesh, and dwelt among us, (and we beheld his glory, the glory as of the only begotten of the Father,) full of grace and truth"* (verse 14).

This revelation changed my life. In the early days of my Christian walk, I delved into the Word of God day and night. I consumed the Scriptures like I would my favorite food. Meditating on the Word of God in that manner has brought me to this conclusion: the Word is truly alive. Hebrews 11:3 says, *"The worlds were framed by the word of God."* For *"word,"* the writer of this epistle used the Greek word *rhema,* which can indicate "a living voice."

God's Word not only speaks to us, but it also speaks in us and through us. The Word of God is meant to be engaged through relationship. Thus, we are to have an intimate relationship with the Word. Jesus said, *"And you shall know the truth, and the truth shall make you free"* (John 8:32). Through the Word, the Creator divulges His mind to humanity. Thus, when we read or hear the Word, we learn the mind of God.

The *rhema* is the word that speaks inside of us. When God illuminates His Word, and it becomes a *rhema* word (alive to us), we experience a revelation. Have you ever read a Bible verse many times, over several years, without really being impacted by it, but then, all of a sudden, the verse just came alive to you? That's a *rhema* word. And the living Word of God is the key to supernatural breakthrough. I desire that God's Word will be living and active inside you, so that you can speak—and live—with power and authority. Today, release your faith and watch God shift your reality.

Day 37: BREAKTHROUGH PRAYER

> Father, in the name of Jesus, I thank You for Your powerful Word. I recognize that Your Word is alive and active; it contains the supernatural, miracle-working power of God, dynamic in its manifestations. I declare Your Word for every situation in my life: *"I shall not die, but live, and declare the works of the LORD."* I am obedient to Your Word; therefore, I will *"eat the good of the land"* all the days of my life. Lord God, I recognize that Your words will never return void, but they will accomplish what You send them to do. I declare that Your words are accomplished in me. Your Word can never fail, has never failed, and will never fail. Your Word declares, *"He that dwells in the secret place of the*

Most High shall abide under the shadow of the Almighty." I declare that I abide in Your Word and therefore dwell in the *"secret place."* The Word is Your will; I delight to hear, meditate on, and obey Your will daily. As I meditate on Your Word, Your wisdom is made manifest in me. I declare that I am a victor through the power of Your Word. In Jesus's name, amen. (See Psalm 118:17; Isaiah 1:19; Isaiah 55:11; Psalm 91:1; Psalm 1:2; Psalm 119:16.)

Day 38: His Power Is Present

And it came to pass on a certain day, as He was teaching, that there were Pharisees and doctors of the law sitting by, which were come out of every town of Galilee, and Judaea, and Jerusalem: and the power of the Lord was present to heal them. (Luke 5:17)

When Jesus walked the earth, He partnered with God's anointing to see miracles manifested. We see an example of this in the situation described above, in which Jesus was teaching, and *"the power of the Lord was present to heal."* I want you to know that the power of the Holy Spirit is present to heal or deliver you from any difficulty you are facing. Yet your ability to receive a miracle is often contingent upon how sensitive you are to the anointing. Once, while I was in the middle of preaching at a particular church, I strongly felt the presence of God, and I began to call people forward for physical healing. The power of God manifested, and many people were healed and delivered. If we are going to live like Jesus, we must be sensitive to the anointing of the Holy Spirit.

You could say that God's power works according to the "law of supply and demand." You must place a claim, or a "demand," upon the anointing. This is what the woman with the flow of blood did when she touched the hem of Jesus's garment. Power went out from Him and into her need, and she was healed. Jesus told her, *"Daughter, be of good comfort: your faith has made you whole; go in peace."* (See Luke 8:43–48.) Begin to ask God to grant you the sensitivity to His Spirit that will allow you to access His power. Whatever the need is, the supply of the Spirit is available to meet it.

Day 38: BREAKTHROUGH PRAYER

Father, in the name of Jesus, I thank You for the anointing of the Holy Spirit. I recognize that Your Spirit is of priceless value. Right now, I release my faith to receive Your supernatural power working in and through my life. Thank You, Father, for the gift of spiritual sensitivity. I believe that Your power is available right now to touch, heal, and deliver me. I receive the dynamic, yolk-destroying, burden-removing power of God and its working right now. My life will never be the same for having been touched by Your anointing. In Jesus's name, amen.

Day 39: Intimacy and Authority

And the evil spirit answered and said, Jesus I know, and Paul I know; but who are you? (Acts 19:15)

I am always amazed when I read the exorcism account in Acts 19. I can remember watching movies about exorcisms when I was growing up. Hollywood's versions of them were very frightening to me. The priest would often talk to the demon and interrogate it, asking all sorts of questions. That type of scenario is what came to my mind the first time I read this account in Scripture. However, this incident from the book of Acts was nothing like that. There was no "interrogation" going on by the people seeking to exorcize the demon. The issue in this passage is that those who commanded the evil spirit to come out in Jesus's name did not know Jesus! They were attempting to use the name and authority of Someone with whom they had no relationship, and that fact was obvious to the evil spirit, who said, "*Jesus I know, and Paul I know; but who are you?*" The moral of the story is that, in Christ, there is an inextricable relationship between intimacy and authority.

Thus, the key to true spiritual authority is intimacy with the person of Jesus Christ and with His Spirit. The greater the intimacy you share with the Holy Spirit, the more of His power will be released in your life. Authority is the right to act in a particular way. Imagine a man walking down the street, seeing another man's wife, and asking her to cook dinner for him when she gets home. That woman probably wouldn't respond positively to such a suggestion. Why? He is not her husband. They don't have an exclusive relationship. Therefore, he doesn't have the right to make such a request. No intimacy, no right.

When we develop an intimate relationship with Jesus, and walk in His authority, the forces of darkness will recognize it and yield to the power of the Spirit working in us.

Day 39: BREAKTHROUGH PRAYER

Father, I recognize that the Holy Spirit desires intimacy with me—and I desire intimacy with Him. I also recognize that Jesus is the living Word. To know the truth is to know the person of Jesus. I delight in Your Word and in Your precepts, day and night. To know You is eternal life; therefore, I declare that the life of God abides within me. Today, I declare that I possess an intimate relationship with God. I desire to spend time in fellowship with the Holy Spirit daily. I exercise His authority in my life, in the name of Jesus. I take authority over every demonic force that would resist my destiny, and I declare supernatural breakthrough over my life. My life will never be the same because I possess an intimate relationship with the Holy Spirit and I release God's supernatural authority over every area of my life. In Jesus's name, amen! (See Psalm 1:2; Psalm 119:16; John 17:3.)

Day 40: Born from Above

For whatsoever is born of God overcomes the world: and this is the victory that overcomes the world, even our faith.

(1 John 5:4)

During a nighttime discourse between Jesus and the Pharisee Nicodemus (see John 3:1–21), Jesus declared that in order to enter the kingdom of God, a person must be *"born again"* (verse 3). In the Greek, this phrase literally means "born from above." I mentioned earlier that I often hear people make the statement, "I am only human." Yes, of course we are human, but if we are believers in Jesus, we have the Spirit of God living in us, and that makes us much more than just human in our potential and capacity. We are born from above if we are in Christ! Being born from above, your rebirth is from another realm. You are born from the very Spirit of God Himself. This means that you are not ordinary—you are extraordinary.

Another maxim I hear people say is "Never forget where you came from." That's good advice. As a Christian, you should never forget where you come from. The Bible says, *"Our citizenship is in heaven"* (Philippians 3:20 NIV). That's right, beloved, your spiritual passport has "heaven" stamped on it as your country of origin. And your heavenly origin enables you to receive breakthrough. Why allow the enemy to rob you of your peace? Why allow yourself to be dominated by fear? Whatever is born of God is destined to overcome the world.

The next time you come across a difficulty or a problem—or even receive a blessing, such as a promotion—I want you to declare, "I was born for this." A fish never questions whether it can swim. A bird never questions whether it can fly. So why do you question whether you can overcome? Your Father is the Creator of the universe—act like it!

Day 40: Breakthrough Prayer

Father, in the name of Jesus, I recognize that You are the author and finisher of my faith. Your Word declares that whoever is born of God overcomes the world; therefore, I declare that I am an overcomer. I was born to be an overcomer. I was born to be victorious. I was born to take dominion over situations and circumstances. I do not cower in the face of my adversary, Satan. I do not fret in the midst of difficulties. I hold my head up high, keeping my shoulders back; I take a stand, and I walk in my spiritual authority. Because of the blood of Jesus Christ and His finished work on the cross, I have a new nature; I am a new creation in Christ. I no longer live in bondage to sin. I am no longer a slave to fear. Today, I release my faith and take my place as a joint-heir with Jesus and a child of the Most High God. In Jesus's name, amen. (See Hebrews 12:2; 1 John 5:4; 2 Corinthians 5:17; Romans 8:17.)

Day 41: Teach Me How to Prosper

Beloved, I wish above all things that you may prosper and be in health, even as your soul prospers. (3 John 1:2)

Have you ever come to the end of yourself? Have you ever been so desperate that you just cried out to God for answers? Years ago, I was in a desperate place in my relationship with God and in my personal finances. At that time, I didn't have the understanding of God's favor and blessings that I do today. I couldn't pay my bills or provide for my family the way I know I should have. One night, out of frustration, I cried out to God, saying, "Teach me how to prosper." That was one of the first times in my life that I had actually acknowledged I didn't know something. When I made that request, something broke inside of me. All of a sudden, I began to receive revelation directly from God. He showed me it was His perfect will for me to prosper in every area of my life. The truth is, until I received that revelation, I didn't really believe that God wanted me to prosper. "Religious" people had taught me that prosperity was a sin, and I had believed it; therefore, for a long time, I couldn't receive the notion that God desired to bless me.

You may be thinking, *You mean to tell me that God wants me to have more than enough?* Absolutely! The Bible says, "*Beloved, I wish above all things that you may prosper and be in health, even as your soul prospers.*" Simply put, God wants you to be whole in every area of your life. The Greek word for "*prosper*" here essentially means to have sufficient resources for the journey. In other words, to live in prosperity is to have everything you need to do everything God has called you to do. When we look at prosperity from this angle, it is clear that the most selfish thing we can do is *not* prosper!

I believe God wants to radically shift your thinking in the same way He shifted mine years ago. He wants to challenge you today to believe Him for more. God desires you to understand that there is no request you can make of Him that will deplete His resources or intimidate Him. I encourage you to ask the same question of the Lord that I asked: "Teach me how to prosper."

Day 41: BREAKTHROUGH PRAYER

Father, in the name of Jesus, I thank You for Your perfect plan of prosperity for my life. I declare that I prosper and am in health, even as my soul prospers. As a result of this prosperity, I am thoroughly furnished and fully supplied to perform every good work that You ordained for me before the foundation of the world. As the seed of Abraham, I declare that there is no lack in my life. The spirit of poverty is destroyed. I have no need of aid or support, but every earthly blessing operates in my life. I daily function from a place of abundance. I declare that all grace abounds toward me—always and in every situation. *"It is more blessed to give than to receive"*; therefore, I declare I am a giver. I am a lender and not a borrower. I am blessed in the city and blessed in the field. Thank You, Lord Jesus, that through Your power, grace, and love, my life is a storehouse for those who have needs. My life is a wellspring of supernatural resources, and I am a distributor of blessings. In Jesus's name, amen. (See Galatians 3:7–9, 14; 2 Corinthians 9:8; Acts 20:35; Deuteronomy 28:3, 12.)

Day 42: Success in the Word

This book of the law shall not depart out of your mouth but you shall meditate therein day and night, that you may observe to do according to all that is written therein: for then you shall make your way prosperous, and then you shall have good success. (Joshua 1:8)

Because God's Word has a central role in breakthrough, I want to reemphasize that one of the first spiritual principles I learned was the importance of meditating on the Word. I learned to meditate on the Scriptures for hours every day, and this spiritual discipline transformed my life. It helped me to lay a strong foundation that is a blessing to me in my life and ministry and will continue to be in the years to come.

What does the Bible mean by "meditate"? The word "*meditate*" in Joshua 1:8 comes from the Hebrew word *hagah*, among whose basic meanings is to speak or mutter something over and over again. Furthermore, the English word *ruminate* comes from a Latin term related to a cow chewing its cud until it can fully digest what it is eating.[1] You and I must do the same thing when it comes to the Word of God. We must speak the Word over and over again until it gets deep down into our spirits. The Bible says that if we meditate on the Word day and night with the desire to do what it says, we will make our way prosperous and we will have good success.

---

1. *Merriam-Webster.com*, 2018, http://www.merriam-webster.com.

Do you want to have good success? The key is learning how to keep God's Word before you constantly. One practical way to do this is to make flashcards with specific Scriptures on them. Then, every day, when you first get up in the morning, read a particular Scripture on a flash card and speak it over and over again. That is how you can begin to frame your day with the Word of God. When God's Word is your heart's desire and your final authority, success is inevitable.

Day 42: BREAKTHROUGH PRAYER

Father, in the name of Jesus, I thank You for the power of Your Word. "*By the word of the LORD were the heavens made; and all the host of them by the breath of His mouth.*" Your Word is the mirror that I look into to affirm my spiritual identity. Moreover, "*Your word is a lamp to my feet, and a light to my path.*" I know that Your Word is the final authority in my life. Everything I need to be successful is wrapped up in the Word. I thank You that as I speak Your Word, it releases supernatural power for victorious living. I walk in victory because the Word is my portion daily. I am who the Word of God says I am. I have what the Word of God says I have. And I can do what the Word of God says I can do. I speak and release Your Word right now, in Jesus's name. Amen. (See Psalm 33:6; Psalm 119:105.)

Day 43: The Hearing of Faith

This only would I learn of you, Received you the Spirit by the works of the law, or by the hearing of faith?

(Galatians 3:2)

One time, I was traveling by plane from Florida to Oklahoma. It was quite a long flight, so I thought I would probably enjoy watching a movie. To my surprise, there were no headsets available on the plane. How was I going to enjoy a movie without any sound? That is the equivalent of what many Christians are doing when they try to enjoy a vibrant relationship with God without exercising faith. The Bible says, "*Without faith it is impossible to please* [God]: *for he that comes to God must believe that He is, and that He is a rewarder of them that diligently seek Him*" (Hebrews 11:6). Just as I wouldn't have been able to fully enjoy the movie without headphones, neither can we see the manifestation of God's power in our lives without faith.

The book of Galatians introduces us to the phrase "*the hearing of faith.*" This tells us our faith has "ears." It hears and receives the Word so we can be transformed. Faith translates the truth and promises of God's Word into a firm foundation upon which we can stand. The context of Galatians 3:2 is that newly converted believers in Galatia were being taught that if they weren't circumcised (an aspect of the Jewish law), they could not be saved. This amounted to basing their salvation on works and not on faith, on God's unmerited favor, and on the power of His

Holy Spirit. We must learn to tap into our spiritual hearing by faith. The moment we hear God's Word and believe is the moment that grace for miracles explodes inside of us.

Everything we need to consciously receive from God comes by faith. Salvation is a work of faith. Healing is a work of faith. Deliverance is a work of faith. Supernatural miracles and breakthroughs don't happen based upon how much head knowledge we possess; they take place by the hearing of faith. Every time we read, study, and speak God's Word, revelation comes. *"Faith comes by hearing, and hearing by the word of God"* (Romans 10:17). Every time the Holy Spirit speaks to us and we act in obedient submission to Him, something is deposited within us to take our capacity to believe to the next level.

Are you ready for your miracle? Stop trying to work your way into the power and presence of God and instead believe your way into the power and presence of God. The Holy Spirit takes the words from the pages of the Bible and breathes on them so that they become life to those who hear them. The enemy of your soul knows the power of faith. That is why he is constantly working overtime to undermine your capacity to believe God. The good news is that the devil has failed. Because of our redemption in Christ, Satan no longer has any legal right to operate in our lives. What are you believing God to do for you today? Whatever it is, simply release your faith and know that if He promised it, He will perform it. (See Romans 4:21.) Let the one who has ears to hear, hear what the Holy Spirit is saying to the church. (See, for example, Revelation 2:7.) Amen.

Day 43: BREAKTHROUGH PRAYER

Father, in the name of Jesus, I thank You that my faith hears You speaking, and Your words are founded in truth. I thank You that, by faith, revelation comes, and as I believe what I hear, the grace for miracles explodes in me. In Your presence is the power to become what You created and redeemed me to be. In Your presence is the power to receive salvation, deliverance, and faith. By my obedience and submission, You make supernatural deposits in my life. I thank You for Your gift of favor and for the hearing of faith, for by them I am able to receive Your promises. In Jesus's name, amen.

Day 44: The Blessing of Abraham

That the blessing of Abraham might come on the Gentiles through Jesus Christ; that we might receive the promise of the Spirit through faith. (Galatians 3:14)

When I attended Sunday school as I was growing up, I would often hear the song about "Father Abraham," which goes:

Father Abraham had many sons,
Many sons had Father Abraham.
I am one of them, and so are you,
So let's just praise the Lord!

At the time, I didn't quite understand how I was connected to Abraham, but the Bible is clear that we are children of Abraham through Jesus Christ. (See, for example, Galatians 3:7–9.) God promised Abraham that his offspring would be "*as numerous as the stars in the sky and as the sand on the seashore*" (Genesis 22:17 NIV). I believe this refers to both natural and spiritual lineage. Abraham was justified by faith before the institution of the Mosaic law with its legal requirements (see, for example, Romans 4:3); thus, being justified by faith is the true spiritual meaning of being a seed of Abraham.

And we have received the blessing of Abraham. Abraham had favor with God. He had a divine connection with the Lord. He was called God's friend. (See 2 Chronicles 20:7; Isaiah 41:8; James 2:23.) He walked in supernatural abundance. All of these things and more are available to every single new-covenant (new-testament) believer. Yet just like any last will and testament, the benefits of this testament cannot be enjoyed until we place a claim, or a demand, upon them. The benefits you fail to claim are the benefits you fail to receive. God wants you to know there is a higher way of living. Are you ready to walk in the blessing? Are you ready for your life to be radically transformed? Are you ready to live in supernatural abundance? To do so, you must understand your identity in Christ. Remember the account in the gospel of Luke of the woman who was so crippled that she was bent over? Jesus healed her, saying, *"Woman, you are set free from your infirmity"* (Luke 13:12 NIV), affirming that she was *"a daughter of Abraham"* (verse 16). Like father, like daughter; or like father, like son. The children should enjoy an even greater manifestation than the father. In Christ Jesus, the blessing of Abraham is on your life. Realize it, receive it, and release it!

Day 44: BREAKTHROUGH PRAYER

Father, I thank You for who You are and for all that You have done in my life. I am a seed of Abraham, and the blessing of Abraham is upon me. Through the blood shed by Your Son Jesus, I am a friend of God, and I receive the promise of the Spirit by faith. I lead a Spirit-led, Spirit-empowered lifestyle. I walk in the faith of my father Abraham, *"who against hope believed in hope"* and became *"the father of many nations."* Every promise You have made to me is true. I embrace the blessing of biblical prosperity. The supernatural favor of God is upon my life, and I operate from that favor daily. Just as You did not hide from Abraham the things You desired to do, neither do You hide Your counsel from me because I am Your friend. I have been justified by faith, and I have peace with God through my Lord and Savior Jesus Christ. *"The just shall live by faith."* I have been justified; therefore, I walk in bold confidence and faith in Your Word. I am not moved by what I see, but I "call those things that are not as though they were," according to Your Word. Thank You for the blessing of Abraham upon my life. In Jesus's name, amen. (See Romans 4:18; Genesis 18:16–18; Romans 5:1; Romans 1:17; Romans 4:17 NIV84.)

Day 45: *Dunamis* Power

And with great power gave the apostles witness of the resurrection of the Lord Jesus: and great grace was upon them all. (Acts 4:33)

One day, as I was cooking in the kitchen, the Holy Spirit spoke to me very clearly, directing my attention to a blender that was on my kitchen counter. The blender was not plugged into the outlet. I heard the Holy Spirit ask me this question: "Kynan, can the blender work in the state that it's in right now?" My answer was, "No." Next, the Lord asked me a follow-up question: "Kynan, why can't that blender work?" I responded, "Because it's not plugged in." The Holy Spirit then said to me that many people in the body of Christ are living a powerless lifestyle because they are not "plugged in."

The Bible says that we will receive power after the Holy Spirit comes upon us. (See Acts 1:8.) Remember that one Greek term translated "*power*"—as in Acts 1:8 and Acts 4:33—is *dunamis*. Again, this is the word from which we derive the English word *dynamite*. Accordingly, every believer has access to dynamic power within them—the power of the Holy Spirit. One purpose of this power is to enable us to bear witness to the resurrection of Jesus.

The Holy Spirit also enables us to live a lifestyle free of sin and bondage. Yet millions of Christians are still living in defeat. Why? They are not plugged into the power source! The Holy Spirit is the power source for Christian living. If you want to live a dynamic Christian life, you must learn to intimately connect with the Holy Spirit. He is the most important Person on the earth—but often the most neglected Person on the earth, in the sense that we don't give Him the attention and devotion He requires.

Do you comprehend that there is a reservoir of spiritual dynamite inside you? Yes! Even more than that, you have a spiritual nuclear reactor within you. Satan is terrified that you will discover the power that lives inside you. Don't ever forget that the same *dunamis* power that raised Jesus from the dead dwells within you. (See Romans 8:11.)

Day 45: BREAKTHROUGH PRAYER

Father, I recognize that Your Spirit, who raised Jesus from the dead, lives inside me. I also recognize that the power of the Holy Spirit gives life to my mortal body. I acknowledge that I have resurrection power dwelling within me. I declare that I am victorious because the Holy Spirit lives inside me. By the power of the Spirit, I break all shackles of shame, defeat, bondage, and iniquity, in the name of Jesus. Sickness, disease, and despair have no power over me. I release the power of the Holy Spirit by faith. I declare that I live a Spirit-led and Spirit-empowered lifestyle. I am not moved by what I see, but I am moved only by the truth of the Word of the Lord. In Jesus's name, amen.

Day 46: The Law of the Spirit of Life

For the law of the Spirit of life in Christ Jesus has made me free from the law of sin and death. (Romans 8:2)

Have you ever heard a Christian use the phrase "We are not under the law"? They say this to quote the apostle Paul (see Romans 6:14) and emphasize that we are not to be governed by legalism in regard to living the Christian life. Although this statement is true, it is incomplete—if those who quote it imply that we're not to be governed by *any* law. The law of Moses has been replaced by a different type of law: we are to live according to *"the law of the Spirit of life in Christ Jesus."* This law has liberated us from *"the law of sin and death."*

"The law of the Spirit of life" is an even higher, more powerful law for righteous living than the law of Moses could ever be. For example, Jesus said that if you look at a woman to lust after her, you've already committed adultery in your heart. (See Matthew 5:28.) That is a deeper responsibility than the law of Moses, which simply stated, *"You shall not commit adultery"* (Exodus 20:14).

Once we receive the Holy Spirit, we have a spiritual law working inside of us. This spiritual law regulates the way we think, act, and function. It's not legalistic—it's relational. If we are operating fully in this law, no one ever has to tell us when we have done something wrong, because the Spirit within us instructs us in right and wrong. In his first epistle, the apostle John wrote that we have received God's anointing within us, and it "*teaches* [us] *of all things*" (1 John 2:27). The Spirit liberates us from the law of sin and death, teaches us to deny ourselves and live in righteousness, and even overrides sickness and disease in our physical bodies. Greater is the One who lives in you than he who is in the world. (See 1 John 4:4.) We are no longer under the law because we have been empowered by grace!

Day 46: BREAKTHROUGH PRAYER

Father, I thank You that "*the law of the Spirit of life in Christ Jesus has made me free from the law of sin and death.*" No longer a slave to sin, I am also no longer bound by sin-consciousness. Your grace has freed me to worship You "*in spirit and in truth.*" The chains of sin, iniquity, and defeat are broken off my life, in the name of Jesus. I declare that the life of the Spirit is working and flowing in me. I declare that no sin or sickness will reign in my mortal body. The natural cells of my body are rejuvenated and regenerated by the power of the Holy Spirit. I believe Your Word, which says that You came so that I might have life and have it more abundantly; therefore, I declare that eternal life is working in me. I desire that You would manifest Your miraculous power. In Jesus's name, amen. (See John 4:23–24; John 10:10.)

Day 47: Divine Strategies for Breakthrough

And Elisha sent a messenger to him, saying, Go and wash in Jordan seven times, and your flesh shall come again to you, and you shall be clean. (2 Kings 5:10)

Many people come to me seeking God's supernatural intervention in their lives—they want God to do a miracle for them. They are not alone. All of us want God to do for us what we cannot seem to do on our own. We want to see His miraculous hand move on our behalf.

Yet while it is true that God is a God of miracles, He is also practical. What do I mean by that? Throughout Scripture, we see that every time God manifested a miracle on someone's behalf, it was because they had obeyed a divine instruction that involved the natural world. This tells me that God is a God of strategy; thus, at times, He will give us the solutions we need in the form of strategies or procedures. These are specific instructions that, once obeyed, cause miraculous things to happen in our lives.

Such was the case with Naaman. This man had an important position as commander of the Syrian army. However, he had a serious problem—he was a leper. Naaman went to the prophet Elisha in Israel seeking a solution. He knew that this man of God was a miracle worker and that the prophet could grant him access to God's supernatural healing. So, you can imagine his frustration when Elisha told him to bathe in the Jordan River seven times. What? The Jordan River? It was one of the filthiest rivers of the day. Yet this was the strategy God had provided for Naaman in order to receive healing and turn his life around.

God will often tell us to do something so simple that following it seems ineffective, so we delay—as did Naaman. But when Naaman finally obeyed the instruction, his leprosy was cleansed instantly. (See 2 Kings 5:1–14.) Similarly, I believe there is a divine strategy that, once implemented, will supernaturally shift your life. It could be as simple as any of these: "Wake up in the morning and pray." "Call this person." "Write this book." "Go to this conference." Whatever it is, if you will simply say, "Here I am, Lord; send me" (see Isaiah 6:8), your life will change forever. Today, ask God to give you the strategy that you need to break through.

Day 47: BREAKTHROUGH PRAYER

Father, I recognize that You are a God of strategy. You know the end from the beginning. You instruct and teach me in the way that I should go. I position myself right now in obedience to You so that You can place Your "super" on my natural. It is clear that I live in the accelerated manifestation of the blessings of God as I obey Your Word. My spirit is receptive to divine strategies, in Jesus's name. I thank You for revelation knowledge flowing in my spirit. Right now, I receive divine strategies for my business, my ministry, my marriage, and my finances. According to Your Word, no weapon formed against me will be able to prosper. Thank You for downloading divine blueprints for success. In Jesus's name, amen. (See Psalm 32:8; Isaiah 54:17.)

Day 48: The Love Factor

For in Jesus Christ neither circumcision avails any thing, nor uncircumcision; but faith which works by love.

(Galatians 5:6)

One of the most popular chapters in the Bible is 1 Corinthians 13, which is often referred to as the Love Chapter. However, what most people don't realize is that the agape love of God is the driving force behind everything in His kingdom. For example, love is literally the energizing power behind faith. Without love, our faith cannot function as God intends. Faith without love is like a car without gasoline: it's going nowhere. Many people are not able to receive the breakthrough that God has for them because their love walk is not intact. At the end of the day, it all comes down to love.

I will never forget the time I bought a car from a dealership, and I drove the car from Fort Lauderdale to Tampa, Florida. On the way, the car began to slow down. Soon, it came to a stop. I couldn't figure out what had happened or what I might have done wrong. I called roadside assistance and waited for nearly an hour before they showed up. To my surprise, the roadside assistant told me that I had run out of gasoline. Because this was a new vehicle and I hadn't known how to read the digital gauge, I hadn't realized the gas tank was that low. The moral of the story is that we must keep our spiritual "tanks" filled with love if we want to fulfill our destinies.

Do you walk in unconditional love? Do you find it easy to forgive people? Do you do good to those who mistreat you? These are the ingredients of supernatural breakthrough. Today, ask God to fill you with His love. As we read in 1 Corinthians 13, love does not think badly of its neighbor. Love is not suspicious, manipulative, or controlling. It is patient, kind, and long-suffering. The more you walk in love, the greater your capacity to receive the blessings God has for you.

Day 48: BREAKTHROUGH PRAYER

Father, You are the Lord of the breakthrough, and Your Word declares that You are love. Therefore, I declare that I walk in the agape love of God. Your Word says that everyone who loves, knows God and is born of God. I declare that I walk in the unconditional love of God toward every person who comes into my life. I freely forgive all who have wronged or hurt me. I release all offenses and trespasses right now. I declare that my spiritual "tank" is filled with love and that I will reach my destination in the name of Jesus. I declare that my enemies are blessed. I do good to those who despitefully use me and persecute me because I am a child of my Father in heaven. Just as You have loved me in the face of my flaws and faults, I look beyond the flaws and faults of others, and I choose to love them unconditionally. I am not fearful or suspicious, because I trust in the power of Your love. My faith is energized today by the agape love of God; therefore, I am positioned to receive my supernatural breakthrough. In Jesus's name, amen. (See 1 John 4:7–8, 16; Matthew 5:44–45.)

Day 49: The Head and Not the Tail

And the Lord *shall make you the head and not the tail; and you shall be above only, and you shall not be beneath; if that you hearken to the commandments of the* Lord *your God which I command you this day, to observe and to do them.* (Deuteronomy 28:13)

God says that we are *"the head and not the tail."* I want you to think about that for moment. What does it actually mean? Many people live their lives underneath situations and circumstances. They allow the things that they have been through and the problems they are currently facing to control them. God promised the Israelites that if they would listen to and obey Him, He would set them *"above only."* The original Hebrew word for this phrase is *ma'al,* one of whose meanings is "on higher ground." God wants us to live on higher ground. It was never in His plan and purpose for His children to merely survive. He said that we would be blessed in the city and blessed in the field. (See Deuteronomy 28:3.) This means more than financial abundance; it refers to a life of victory and purpose. If you're going to experience breakthrough, you must know exactly where you belong.

Years ago, when people were in a good place financially or when good things happened to them, they would say, "I'm living on top of the world." Although this was a secular expression, it describes the way God intends for His children to live. In no way does this statement imply superiority to other people.

However, it does imply superiority to the devil. In Jesus, we have been given *"power…over all the power of the enemy"* (Luke 10:19). Regardless of what you face today, know that the God whom you serve is a God of elevation and promotion. The God whom you serve lifts you out of the pit of depression and places you in the palace of purpose. It is time to take your place at the top today!

Day 49: BREAKTHROUGH PRAYER

Father, You said in Your Word that You would make me "the head and not the tail; above only, and not beneath." Therefore, I declare that I am the head over my situations and circumstances. I am not the tail, nor am I beneath. I live above the mental and emotional attacks of the enemy. I live above depression and despair. I live above anxiety and fear. Your Word declares in Genesis 1:26 that You created us to have dominion; therefore, I declare that I am a dominion-heir. Deuteronomy 8:18 declares that You give us the power to obtain wealth to establish Your covenant; therefore, my mind and my hands are receptive to creativity and wealth-generating ideas. I live a thriving and prosperous life according to the will of God. I am not selfish or self-promoting, but I am thoroughly convinced that You are a good God and You desire good things for me. I am unapologetic about the prosperity released into my life. In Jesus's name, amen.

Day 50: Your Will Be Done

Your kingdom come. Your will be done in earth, as it is in heaven. (Matthew 6:10)

One of the most complex aspects of the human experience is the human will. This attribute is seemingly paradoxical. On the one hand, God created us in His image for His glory and pleasure, and we owe loyalty and obedience to Him; on the other hand, when He created us, He gave us free will. Why? He wanted us to have free moral agency. This simply means we have the ability to make our own choices. Our soul is comprised of three parts—mind, will, and emotions—and the will is what drives our decisions.

At the center of God's desire for His kingdom to come on the earth is that His will would be done. Sometimes, our will clashes with God's will. How do we rectify this tension? We learn to submit our wills to His. Contrary to popular opinion, God does not desire for us to *give up* our wills. If we did that, we would no longer be free moral agents. Instead, He desires for us to *yield* our wills to His. This means that we must make a conscious decision to deny our desires when they conflict with His.

The will of God can be known through the Word of God. The more we meditate on God's Word, the more we will understand His will. Accordingly, if you are going to pray for God's intervention and supernatural breakthrough in your life according to His Word, you must understand what the Word of the Lord says. It amazes me that so many people are ignorant concerning the will of God for their lives. As a result, they don't know how to pray appropriately—or how to live in the fullness of life He desires to give. For example, if you know it is the will of God that you walk in divine health, you will never accept sickness as something sent from God. If you know it is the will of God for you to be the head and not the tail, you will never accept defeat or depression as His purpose for you. When we discover God's will, we discover His purposes, and when we know His purposes, we can tap into His power. Many people are frustrated that they cannot advance in the kingdom of God. They are upset at the stagnation they are experiencing in their lives. Yet one of the keys to overcoming stagnation is learning how to submit to the sovereignty of God. Allow Him to take control of your life. Stop making decisions that are contrary to His Word. Say, "Lord, Your will be done on earth as it is in heaven." The moment you make this conscious decision, breakthrough is yours.

Day 50: BREAKTHROUGH PRAYER

Father, I recognize that it is not my will but Your will that needs to be done in my life and in the earth. Let Your kingdom have its full expression within me. Let Your purpose and power flow through my life in a way that is pleasing to You. I submit my thoughts, desires, and decisions to the counsel of Your Word. I declare that Your Word is the final authority in my life. When You tell me to speak, I will speak. When You tell me to be silent, I will be silent. It is my pleasure to worship and obey You. Thank You for being my Good Shepherd and the Bishop of my soul. In Jesus's name, amen. (See John 10:11, 14; 1 Peter 2:25.)

Day 51: As for Me and My Whole House

And if it seem evil to you to serve the Lord, choose you this day whom you will serve; whether the gods which your fathers served that were on the other side of the flood, or the gods of the Amorites, in whose land you dwell: but as for me and my house, we will serve the Lord. (Joshua 24:15)

Jesus said, "*In my Father's house are many mansions: if it were not so, I would have told you. I go to prepare a place for you*" (John 14:2). When I was growing up, I would often hear people quote this verse from the gospel of John. They would say things like, "I have a mansion in heaven." Though that is a very exciting idea, it is not exactly what Jesus was referring to here. The Greek word translated "*mansion*" means "dwelling place" and indicates "a family."[2] Furthermore, in ancient times, when a certain Hebrew term was used for *house*, it referred to a family or community—for example, the house of Jacob, the house of David, and the house of Israel. It always indicated familial tribes or communities. It was the term Joshua used when he said, "*As for me and my house, we will serve the Lord.*"

In the New Testament, a certain nobleman traveled to see Jesus in order to receive a miracle for his son, who was dying. (See John 4:46–53.) Jesus told him to go his way, for his son was healed. On the nobleman's way home, he met his servants coming to meet him, and they told him his son was alive. When he asked what time his son had gotten better, they told him it

2. See, for example, https://www.gotquestions.org/mansions-heaven.html.

was at a certain hour the day before. *"So the father knew that it was at the same hour, in the which Jesus said to him, Your son lives: and himself believed, and his whole house"* (verse 53). Salvation came to the entire house of this nobleman because he believed in Jesus.

I declare that salvation is coming to your entire household in the name of Jesus. Not just your immediate family, but everybody connected to you, will be saved, healed, and delivered by the power of the Holy Spirit. You must stand on this promise; you must believe it with all of your heart. Joshua spoke on the behalf of his family when he said that he and his entire house would serve the Lord. Make that your declaration today. Declare that your entire household will serve the Lord!

Day 51: BREAKTHROUGH PRAYER

Father, when Paul and Silas were imprisoned and You miraculously freed them, they told the jailor of the prison, *"Believe on the Lord Jesus Christ, and you shall be saved, and your house."* Additionally, Joshua declared that he and his entire household would serve the Lord. Therefore, I declare that not only myself, but also my entire household, will be saved and serve You with all our hearts. We will not worship any idols, including money and fame. I declare that we will not be bound or afflicted all the days of our lives. Instead, we will enjoy a covenant relationship with You and be covenant-keepers, because we serve a covenant-keeping God. I declare a blessing over my entire household right now. My household is healed, my household is delivered, and my household is restored. I stand in proxy on behalf of my entire family. Father, let Your will be done in my house. In Jesus's name, amen. (See Acts 16:31.)

Day 52: Blessed to Be a Blessing

> *I have showed you all things, how that so laboring you ought to support the weak, and to remember the words of the Lord Jesus, how He said, "It is more blessed to give than to receive."* (Acts 20:35)

When my second daughter was just a little bitty girl, we began to teach her about giving, and I remember a funny experience in connection with that process. We would encourage her (and her siblings) to put money in the offering basket by providing her with some money in advance and telling her to give it to the church as a tithe or an offering. One day, my daughter went to the basket and put in some money; shortly afterward, she took the money back out. When we asked her what she was doing, she said, "I gave it to God, but He didn't take it, so I took it back."

Many people in the church approach giving in the same way my daughter did when she was just a child. They don't understand the purpose or the process of giving. Unfortunately, recent statistics show that only about 6 percent of churchgoing Christians in the United States actually tithe on a regular basis.[3] The truth is that giving is one of the greatest opportunities for breakthrough and blessing that we have in the kingdom of God. Jesus told us that "*it is more blessed to give than to receive.*" You are blessed to be a blessing. The moment you posture yourself

---

3. See, for example, https://www.sharefaith.com/blog/2015/12/facts-christians-tithing/; https://www.aol.com/article/finance/2015/04/03/do-only-rich-folks-tithe/21159958/.

in this way is the moment the floodgates of heaven will begin to open in your life in ways that you've never imagined before.

The earth contains vast resources, and I would imagine it is God's desire for those resources to be stewarded by people who know Him. Learning financial and stewardship principles from the Bible has radically reshaped my life and ministry. In an earlier devotional, I described how there was a time when I was not able to prosper the way the Bible said I should, and I could not understand why. God began to show me there were areas of selfishness in my life preventing me from giving to the degree He desired me to give. When I began to change my thinking in this area, I experienced breakthrough in my life. The law of the seed is very real. The harvest is always hidden in the seed. If we would only learn to allow God's resources to flow freely through our hands and bless others, we would receive more and more resources to do the work God wants us to do. As I expressed earlier, the most selfish thing a believer can do is to refuse to prosper! Are you ready to be a blessing today?

Day 52: BREAKTHROUGH PRAYER

Father, like the patriarch Abraham, I am blessed to be a blessing. I declare that the blessing of Abraham is upon my life, and, as a result, I am in a position to help others according to Your will. Today, I take the mandate of being a blessing seriously. I declare that my life and my resources are available to advance Your kingdom. I will not hoard resources for myself; instead, I will be a divine distributor of heaven's storehouse. Use me to help someone who cannot help themselves. I want to be a vessel of honor who demonstrates Your generosity in the earth. I declare that I lack nothing in my life. I declare that You supply all my needs according to Your riches in glory. I live from a place of abundance. The works of my hands prosper according to Your will. I am a resource in Your kingdom to bring people into a consciousness of Jesus Christ. In Jesus's name, amen! (See Genesis 12:2–3; 2 Timothy 2:21; Philippians 4:19.)

Day 53: Supernatural Favor

For You, Lord, will bless the righteous; with favor will you compass him as with a shield. (Psalm 5:12)

The psalmist David wrote that the Lord *"will bless the righteous"* person, and will surround that person with favor. For all of my Christian life, I have experienced the favor of God in some way or another. God's favor includes His goodwill, benevolence, grace, and power. Having His hand upon us makes all the difference. It makes us distinct from the crowd. When we're walking in God's favor, people will do things for us that they don't do for everyone else.

One time, a very expensive laptop that I owned was stolen, so my wife and I began to pray. Two weeks later, with no police report ever having been filed, someone from the sheriff's department showed up at our door with the laptop, telling us it had been found twenty miles away. It was not damaged at all. This was the favor of God in manifestation.

Although this is an excellent example of God's favor, the ultimate expression of receiving His favor is to be in Christ Jesus. The moment we are born again, we become a part of the beloved community of God. (See Ephesians 1:6.) We have been given the same favor with the heavenly Father that rests upon Jesus. What does such great favor look like? It looks like tremendous blessing in every area of our lives, including walking in miracles and living in biblical prosperity.

The Lord surely encompasses us with favor as with a shield. Declare that something good is going to happen in your life today in which you will experience unusual favor. Receive God's favor today and live as a child of the King!

Day 53: BREAKTHROUGH PRAYER

Father, I believe You have blessed me with favor. Under the banner of favor, I have already received Your grace and power. I know that I am a member of Your community of the beloved. The grace and favor You extend to Jesus as Your beloved Son is the same grace and favor that manifests in my life by the Spirit of God because I am Your child and a co-heir with Jesus. I decree that divine favor is mine, and, as a result, I will experience unusual blessings and opportunities. Something good is going to happen to me today. Thank You, Jesus! Favor is mine! In the name of Jesus, amen.

Day 54: Arise and Shine

Arise, shine; for your light is come, and the glory of the L*ORD* *is risen upon you.* (Isaiah 60:1)

I believe this is the greatest hour for the church in human history. I know that is a very bold statement, but I believe it is absolutely true. However, it cannot become a collective reality until it becomes a reality for individual believers. Thus, it is just as much your time to shine as an individual believer as it is for the church as a whole.

The church will shine with the light of Christ like never before. The Bible tells us that God wants a *"glorious"* bride, without *"spot," "wrinkle,"* or *"blemish."* (See Ephesians 5:27.) In other words, Jesus is not coming back for a church that is "busted and disgusted." He is coming back for a victorious church that radiates the brightness of the kingdom of God.

The book of Isaiah says, *"Arise, shine; for your light is come, and the glory of the* L*ORD* *is risen upon you."* And Jesus told us, *"Let your light so shine before men, that they may see your good works, and glorify your Father which is in heaven"* (Matthew 5:16). God is waiting for us to reveal His glory to the nations of the earth!

Right now, you may be in a posture of despair or a position of despondency. If so, the Spirit of the Lord is saying to you, "Arise and shine!" It is time for the church to wake up from its spiritual slumber and apathy. It is time for us to become the glorious bride that Christ says we already are. This is not the time to sit down and be defeated; this is the time to rise up and take our place in the kingdom of God. Your season of defeat is over. Your season of despair has come to a close. This is your time to shine!

Day 54: BREAKTHROUGH PRAYER

Father, I know that You are good and Your mercy endures forever. I declare that from this day forward, I arise and shine according to Your Word. I refuse to remain in darkness. I choose today to allow Your glorious light to shine in and through me. I *"cast off the works of darkness, and...put on the armor of light."* I declare that I am Your candlestick, and I will burn brightly for Your glory. I declare that prosperity, increase, and abundance belong to me. I will never be afraid of what the future holds for me. I choose to rejoice in the power of Your Word. I release my faith now for miracles, signs, and wonders. I declare that all areas of compromise, confusion, and disorder are removed from my life right now. *"Your word is a lamp to my feet, and a light to my path."* I declare that Your supernatural light shines through me to the nations, in the name of Jesus! Amen. (See Jeremiah 33:11; Romans 13:12; Psalm 119:105.)

Day 55: Behold, I Do a New Thing

Behold, I will do a new thing; now it shall spring forth; shall you not know it? I will even make a way in the wilderness, and rivers in the desert. (Isaiah 43:19)

I have heard it said that the only constant in life is change. That statement is very true. However, there is an even greater reality: the fact that God is a God of new beginnings. I have often said that "God lives in the now, and to live in the now is to live in the new." God is a God of new beginnings, new dreams, new blessings, and new opportunities. Are you ready for God to do something new in your life?

The word of the Lord came to Isaiah the prophet, saying, "*Behold, I will do a new thing.... I will even make a way in the wilderness, and rivers in the desert.*" I believe the "*way in the wilderness*" represents God opening supernatural doors in our lives—doors that defy reason and logic. "*Rivers in the desert*" refers to God turning every dry place in our lives into a fertile and prosperous place.

We must be sensitive to the new things God is doing and not get stuck in the trap of dwelling on the past. Many people focus on the past, and, as a result, they miss the new thing God is doing. This was the problem the Pharisees had when the Messiah came to earth in the person of Jesus. They were so caught up in the old ways that they could not recognize the new—which was actually the fulfillment of the old.

One of the keys to breakthrough is learning how to embrace your new season. If you will dare to embrace the new and live in the now, without dwelling on or being stuck in the past, God will bring you into the manifestation of His supernatural promises for your life. Bible says, *"If any man be in Christ, he is a new creature: old things are passed away; behold, all things are become new"* (2 Corinthians 5:17). It doesn't matter what you have experienced up to this point—things are changing for the better. The glory of the Lord will be revealed in your life!

Day 55: BREAKTHROUGH PRAYER

Father, I recognize that You are the God of new beginnings. I embrace the new right now. You said that You would make a way in the wilderness and rivers in the desert; therefore, I believe that my season of prosperity is now. I release the past. I choose to let go of negative experiences. I choose not to dwell on toxic emotions. I give all those things to You, and by faith, I step into newness of life. I declare that I have a renewed vision of the future and will not look back. In Jesus's name, amen! (See Romans 6:4.)

Day 56: Free Indeed

If the Son therefore shall make you free, you shall be free indeed. (John 8:36)

What is freedom? For some people, it means experiencing joy occasionally. For others, it means the ability to manage their own lives. For still others, it means doing whatever they feel like. Many people settle for appearing to be free on the outside but remaining bound on the inside. Beloved, that is not God's idea of freedom. Imagine a prisoner being released from jail, only to be bound again days after his release. Is he free? Of course not. We must have a freedom that *lasts*.

Jesus said, *"And you shall know the truth, and the truth shall make you free"* (John 8:32). Real freedom begins with knowing the truth and extends to the transformation that truth produces within us as it renews our minds and hearts. Real freedom is the ability to serve God without hindrance—it can never be negated by our circumstances. Real freedom is the ability to worship God *"in spirit and in truth"* (John 4:23).

I believe it is time for the church to experience true and lasting freedom. Once we have been set free, we never need to go back into bondage again. Most of us wouldn't make the same mistakes we made when we were younger. Would you make the same poor decisions you made as a teenager, for example? That would be a very miserable experience. Why wouldn't you make those mistakes again? Because of what you know now. Your life experiences and the counsel of others have taught you a better way. Similarly, the knowledge of the truth of our life in Christ empowers us to make the right decisions and operate from a place of freedom. God's Word liberates us from bondage. "*You shall know the truth, and the truth shall make you free.*" You no longer have to be bound by sin, iniquity, addictions, lust, fear, pride, poverty, or sickness. You can be set free today. Because the Son has made you free, you are free indeed!

Day 56: BREAKTHROUGH PRAYER

Father, Your Word declares that if the Son makes me free, I am free indeed. Therefore, I declare that I am truly free, in the name of Jesus. I'm no longer a slave to sin. I'm no longer in bondage to my past. Your Word is truth, and that truth empowers and liberates me right now. As a new creation in Christ Jesus, I cannot do the negative things I did before. I cannot say certain things I said before. I cannot go to some of the places I went to before. The old me has been put to death with Christ on the cross, and the new me has been resurrected with Christ and empowered to "*walk in newness of life.*" Thank You, Lord Jesus, for paying the ultimate price to make me free. Because of my freedom in You, I will serve God and worship Him "*in spirit and in truth.*" I declare that I am free indeed! In Jesus's name, amen. (See John 17:17; 2 Corinthians 5:17; Colossians 3:1–4; Romans 6:4–14.)

Day 57: The Way Maker

And Moses said to the people, Fear you not, stand still, and see the salvation of the L*ORD*, *which He will show to you to day.* (Exodus 14:13)

Have you ever been in a situation that was so difficult you couldn't see any way out of it? Have you ever been surrounded by problems that were too big for you? Have you ever felt like the situation you were in was impossible to overcome? Then you are a prime candidate to meet the Way Maker!

After being freed from slavery in Egypt, the Israelites found themselves at a dead end. The Red Sea was in front of them and the Egyptian army was pursuing them. There was nowhere to go! Yet God specializes in impossible situations. He told Moses to instruct the children of Israel to stand still and see His salvation. With just a lifting of his staff, Moses introduced the children of Israel to the Way Maker and the Miracle Worker. The Red Sea parted in the middle, and they walked through it on dry ground. (See Exodus 14.)

You might not be in front of the physical Red Sea, but you might be facing a very difficult situation. The God of wonders desires to show Himself strong on your behalf. He is simply looking for someone who will believe in Him and obey what He says to do. If you will seek God with your whole heart, He will show you just how real He is.

I declare that the crooked paths in your life are about to become straight. The mountains are about to be made low. The rough places are about to be made plain. The desert is about to become a river. (See Isaiah 40:4; 43:19.) Today is your day for miracles!

Day 57: BREAKTHROUGH PRAYER

Father, I believe that You are the Way Maker and the Miracle Worker. You are the One who opens doors that no one can close, and closes doors that no one can open. Your Word declares that all things are possible to those who believe; therefore, I believe in the power of Your Word. With one blast of Your nostrils, you can split a sea in half. You placed the stars in the universe, and You set the boundaries of the earth. I declare that every difficult situation in my life turns around, for the glory of God. I declare that every sickness is healed and every problem is solved by the power of the Holy Spirit. From this day forward, I will never be bound again. I declare that miracles are my portion. In Jesus's name, amen. (See Isaiah 22:22; Mark 9:23; Isaiah 45:12; Psalm 74:17.)

Day 58: Divine Recovery

And David inquired at the Lord, saying, Shall I pursue after this troop? shall I overtake them? And He answered him, Pursue: for you shall surely overtake them, and without fail recover all. (1 Samuel 30:8)

One of my favorite hobbies is collecting pens. I vividly remember acquiring a very expensive pen—and then losing it! I was very upset and frustrated by the loss of this pen, but despite all of my efforts, I couldn't find it. Years later, I went to the glove compartment of my car to look for something else, and lo and behold, there was my pen! I couldn't believe it. Although I was excited and grateful to recover the pen, I received something much greater: God spoke to me through this situation and told me that everything that had been lost in my life would be recovered.

David had a much more serious loss in his life, which is recorded in 1 Samuel 30. He and his men came back from battle one day to find their entire camp had been pillaged and burned by the Amalekites. Furthermore, the women, children, and everyone else left in the camp had been captured. The situation was so devastating that the men in David's army considered stoning him. But the Bible says that *"David encouraged himself in the Lord his God"* (1 Samuel 30:6). Not only did he encourage himself, but he went further and inquired of the Lord about what he should do in response to this shocking situation. God answered and told David he should pursue—and would recover all.

I believe you, too, are about to recover all in your life. Whatever has been lost, defrauded from you, or stolen will be restored. You have to make a decision that you are willing to recover what belongs to you. Many Christians sit back and allow the enemy to take things from them without a fight. However, in this season, if you are *"willing and obedient, you shall eat the good of the land"* (Isaiah 1:19). You will experience the grace of God in a way you have never experienced it before. One meaning of *recover* is to get back to a place of full use and utility. God's hand of recovery and restoration will be revealed in your life!

Day 58: BREAKTHROUGH PRAYER

Father, I know that You are the God of restoration. Everything that was lost, stolen, or defrauded from me will be restored, in the name of Jesus. Just as David pursued the Amalekites and recovered all, I will pursue everything the enemy has taken from me, and I will recover all. I declare that finances are restored. I declare that dreams are restored. I declare that relationships that have been established and ordained by God are restored. I declare that my ministry is restored. I declare that my emotions are fully recovered. This is my season of divine restoration. In Jesus's name, amen!

Day 59: Financial Justice

I will restore their fortunes, and will have mercy on them.
(Jeremiah 33:26 AMP)

To say that God is a God of justice would be an understatement. David said, *"Justice and judgment are the habitation of Your throne"* (Psalm 89:14). Furthermore, the love of God and the justice of God are inseparable, as the second half of this verse from the Psalms indicates: *"mercy and truth shall go before Your face"* (verse 14). Can you imagine a husband watching his wife be physically assaulted or abused by another man and doing nothing about it? Can you imagine him telling her, "Honey, I love you, but I don't involve myself in those kinds of situations"? Does he really love her? The answer to that question is obvious. How, then, could anyone suggest that God would sit back and watch His children suffer such things as financial loss due to abuse or defraudation without doing anything about it? Jesus taught the parable of the unjust judge, in which He concluded, *"And shall not God avenge his own elect, which cry day and night to Him, though He bear long with them? I tell you that He will avenge them speedily"* (Luke 18:7–8).

I believe that God wants you to experience financial justice. By this, I mean God wants to compensate you for everything the enemy has stolen in regard to your finances—even financial issues in your bloodline, going back generations, that have never been resolved. But you must receive financial justice by faith and place a demand on it. As I have shared this concept throughout the world, I have seen hundreds, if not thousands, of people experience financial recovery. People have seen businesses restored and monies found that they never knew existed—all because of the revelation that God is a God of financial justice.

Do you believe God is more than capable of restoring everything the devil has defrauded from you? The Judge of all the universe is waiting for you to approach His throne today and ask.

Day 59: BREAKTHROUGH PRAYER

Father, I thank You that You are the just Judge of all the earth. You hold the entire universe in Your hand. The Bible declares that the silver and gold belong to You, and You own the cattle on a thousand hills. I know it is not Your will that Your people suffer financial bondage or lack. Therefore, I decree and declare financial justice in every area of my life. I declare that everything that was defrauded from me must be restored today, in Jesus's name. I declare that the spirit of financial debt is broken off of my life. I declare that all stolen or swindled contracts, lands, properties, businesses, and connections be restored right now by the courts of heaven. I reverse every injunction of the enemy against anything God has promised me. In Jesus's name, amen! (See Genesis 18:25; Haggai 2:8; Psalm 50:10.)

Day 60: The Spirit of Restoration

"For I will make you a name and a praise among all the peoples of the earth when I restore your fortunes [and freedom] before your eyes," says the Lord.

(Zephaniah 3:20 AMP)

To continue the theme of the last few days, I want to encourage you once again that God desires to restore everything you have lost. I know something about being restored. There was a season in my life when I truly thought I would never rise again. But the Lord brought hope and restoration. It is clear that the entire redemptive plan of God was to restore the human race to intimate fellowship with Himself and the life of abundance He planned for us to enjoy. Yet many professing Christians find it difficult to believe that God truly desires to bring healing and restoration to their lives.

Are you broken? Disappointed? Hurt? You can be restored! Maybe you have lost a relationship, a position, or a valuable possession. I have good news for you—it's not over. Things are turning around for you. You can begin again in the name of Jesus. No matter what harm the enemy has done in your life, if you will surrender to the God of restoration, He will renew you. When something is restored, it is brought back to a state of newness or vibrancy. In Matthew 12, Jesus encountered a man with a withered hand. We don't know what caused this condition, but only that one of his hands was not functioning. The Scripture says, "*Then says He* [Jesus] *to the man, Stretch forth your hand. And he stretched it forth; and it was restored whole, like as the other"* (verse 13). We, too, can reach out to God and allow Him to restore us to wholeness.

When we experience real restoration, we no longer look like the pain and circumstances we have walked through. *"If any man be in Christ, he is a new creature: old things are passed away; behold, all things are become new"* (2 Corinthians 5:17). Are you ready for a new season? Are you ready for a new you? Today is your day of restoration!

Day 60: BREAKTHROUGH PRAYER

Father, I thank You for who You are and all that You have done in my life. Today is the day of restoration! I walk in the favor of God. I am distinct from the people around me, and I walk in grace and preferential treatment. Doors are opened to me supernaturally. I am a magnet of divine favor and supernatural blessings. Everything that was lost, stolen, defrauded, or forfeited is restored today by the power of the Holy Spirit. Everywhere I go today, someone will be used by God to do extraordinary things for me. The doors of promotion and increase are opened to me. I will receive both natural and spiritual gifts today. Heavenly Father, I will no longer be trapped in spiritual barrenness or defeat but will flourish and prosper according to Your will. I declare that today is the day of the Lord's favor. I will meet someone today who will favor me financially. People are prompted to do wonderful things for me. All grace abounds toward me in a way that causes me to have all sufficiency in all areas of my life. Health, favor, relationships, finances, and peace are restored to me now, in the name of Jesus. Amen! (See 2 Corinthians 9:8.)

Day 61: The Children's Bread

I have been young, and now am old; yet have I not seen the righteous forsaken, nor his seed begging bread.

(Psalm 37:25)

Previously, we looked at the account from Matthew 15:21–28 of the Syro-Phoenician woman who boldly approached Jesus and asked Him if He would heal her daughter. Jesus replied, in effect, "It is not fit to give the children's bread to dogs." I believe that if many Christians had been in her shoes, they would have converted to another religion at this point! However, the woman persisted in her faith, replying, *"Truth Lord: yet the dogs eat of the crumbs which fall from their masters' table"*—and she received the miracle she was seeking.

This is an amazing account of faith and courage. However, there is another dynamic to the story that we often overlook. Jesus referred to something called the *"children's bread."* What does that mean? The "children's bread" was an idiomatic expression that referred to the promises and blessings given to the children of Abraham. In other words, as descendants of Abraham, the Jewish people were entitled to healing, deliverance, breakthrough, and prosperity. Today, all of us who have put our faith in Christ are entitled to the same thing—and even greater blessings because we are the spiritual descendants of Abraham. (See Romans 4:11–13.) In essence, healing is not just something God "might" do for us if He is so inclined, but healing is the birthright of every believer. The same is true of any other promise in the Word of God, including deliverance, prosperity, and peace of mind.

However, if healing, deliverance, and prosperity are the children's bread, then why are so many of God's people living beneath their birthright? I believe that most Christians are not experiencing the full manifestation of their spiritual heritage in Christ. They don't realize they are, in fact, the children of Abraham and therefore heirs of the promise. Beloved, stop settling for scraps—it is time for you to eat at the Master's table!

Day 61: BREAKTHROUGH PRAYER

Father, I thank You for Your goodness and grace toward me. I declare that I am a seed of Abraham; therefore, I am entitled to the children's bread. I receive my healing, deliverance, breakthrough, peace, and prosperity in the name of Jesus Christ. I declare that I will no longer settle for scraps and crumbs, but I will eat at the Father's table. I will never allow the enemy to talk me out of my birthright again. I declare that I am blessed, healed, delivered, and made whole by the blood of Jesus Christ. I walk in the fullness of God, because I am an heir of God, and a joint-heir with Jesus. I am part of God's royal family. I will never think, perceive, or behave like a pauper, because I am a king and a priest unto God through the blood of Jesus Christ. Thank You, Lord, for Your faithfulness in my life. I thank You that my family members are consecrated to You through my profession of faith in the name of Jesus. I sanctify my children, other family members and loved ones, coworkers, and neighbors to Your divine purpose for their lives. I walk in the blessing of Abraham all the days of my life. In the name of Jesus, amen! (See Romans 8:17; Revelation 1:6; 5:10.)

Day 62: Extravagant Grace

For by grace are you saved through faith; and that not of yourselves: it is the gift of God. (Ephesians 2:8)

If there is one thing of which I am certain, it is that God is a God of abundant grace. I am a living witness of this truth. However, I believe that the church is extremely ill-informed when it comes to the grace of God. Some people see the message of grace as a dangerous application of Scripture because they are reacting to those who interpret that message as a license to sin. Thus, they emphasize that our teaching on grace must always be balanced with teaching on the fear of God. In a sense, they are both right and wrong. The message of grace has never been and will never be a license to sin. On the contrary, Paul wrote, *"Shall we continue in sin, that grace may abound? God forbid"* (Romans 6:1–2). Nevertheless, a message about grace does not always require balance with a message about the fear of God if it is properly understood. We must realize that the ethos of the gospel is the grace of God. In His benevolence, God sacrificed Himself to save us. This was not about our inherent goodness or righteousness, but rather the inevitable result of His loving-kindness toward us.

God's grace encompasses much more than many people realize. The Bible tells us that *"by grace are you saved through faith; and that not of yourselves: it is the gift of God."* The word *"grace"* here refers to God's gifts of unmerited favor, goodness, and enabling power. God's grace is His favor toward us. However, it is also the empowerment and holy influence of God in our lives.

You are favored by God! I want you to allow that truth to sink in for a moment. God loves you more than you can imagine, and He has supplied you with His inexhaustible grace—His extravagant grace. (See, for example, 2 Corinthians 9:8.) Yes, God paid the ultimate price to bring us into relationship with Himself, but do you think His grace runs out after you become a believer? Never! His grace enables us to live a supernatural life and walk in victory. It empowers us to deny ourselves and the things of the flesh in order to live a life that is pleasing to the Father. It allows us to daily receive the good things that are freely given to us by God. (See 1 Corinthians 2:12.) It is time for the church to receive the manifold grace of God, which releases supernatural breakthrough in our lives. I believe an awakening is coming to the body of Christ that will bring us into a consciousness of the full grace of God.

Day 62: BREAKTHROUGH PRAYER

Father, I recognize that Your grace is extravagant and inexhaustible. You love me with a steadfastness that I cannot comprehend. Even so, I receive this truth that You love me unconditionally. Your grace empowers me to walk righteously and to do those things that are pleasing in Your sight. I declare that my mind is renewed by the power of Your Word and my life is transformed according to Your divine pattern. I have been forgiven on the basis of Christ's sacrifice for me; therefore, I declare that I am the righteousness of God in

Christ Jesus. I am a new creation in Christ; therefore, *"old things are passed away; behold, all things are become new."* In Jesus's name, amen! (See 1 John 3:22; 2 Corinthians 5:21; 2 Corinthians 5:17.)

Day 63: Miracle in Your Mouth

But what says it? The word is near you, even in your mouth, and in your heart: that is, the word of faith, which we preach. (Romans 10:8)

Over the years, research has been conducted on the power of sound. It has been discovered that sound has the ability to cause form within matter, to create and maintain form. A device was developed called a CymaScope, which measures the effect that sound has on the shape of matter.[4] Similarly, our words have the power to shape our world. Yet millions of people all over the globe are ignorant of the miracle that is in their mouth. That's right, beloved: your breakthrough is in your mouth.

The Bible says, *"Death and life are in the power of the tongue"* (Proverbs 18:21). How seriously do we take that Scripture? Do we really believe we will live in the reality that our words create? If we knew that every word was a seed that would produce an exponential harvest, would we continue to say the things we have been saying? *"You shall also decree a thing, and it shall be established to you"* (Job 22:28).

This truth has challenged me in ways I cannot begin to describe. I realize that many battles I have faced in my life were created by words I spoke. Conversely, many blessings I have experienced came from words I spoke. I want to challenge you today to change the way you think and speak so you can change

4. See, for example, https://ted.com/talks/evan_grant_cymatics?utm_source=tedcomshare&utm_medium=email&utm_campaign=tedspread; http://mindinmotion.co.za/sound-affects-matter/; http://www.cymascope.com/cymascope.html.

the way you live. Some people dismiss this principle as "name it and claim it" theology. But Jesus said that the words He spoke were *"spirit"* and *"life"* (John 6:63), and they can continue to be that for us as we speak His words. From this moment on, I want you to steward the miracle in your mouth. Declare God's Word over your life. Decree His promises over your family.

Did you know that when the Scriptures speak of a blessing, more often than not, they are referring to an oral blessing from the mouth of a patriarch to his family? Declare today that you are blessed. Whatever you are believing God to do, begin to speak it with your mouth. Those are not idle words if they are the words of God—they are pregnant with miracle power.

Day 63: BREAKTHROUGH PRAYER

Father, Your Word declares, "*Death and life are in the power of the tongue: and they that love it shall eat the fruit thereof.*" You have said that the word is near to me, even in my mouth, which is the word of faith. I speak the word of faith right now, and I believe I will see the manifestation of what You have promised. I declare that Your miraculous power is flowing in my life. Today, I will experience miracles, signs, and wonders. The unusual favor of God is upon me; therefore, doors open for me supernaturally. I declare that I am healed—from the crown of my head to the souls of my feet. I declare that the blessing of Abraham is upon my life. I declare that I live in the miraculous every day. I ask You to release the miracle in my mouth right now. In Jesus's name, amen. (See Genesis 12:2–3.)

Day 64: The Law of the Seed

While the earth remains, seedtime and harvest, and cold and heat, and summer and winter, and day and night shall not cease. (Genesis 8:22)

One of the most important principles you will ever learn is the principle of seedtime and harvest. Everything that exists in the earth existed in seed form before it came into manifestation. As noted earlier, this is what is called the law of the seed. Remember, the harvest is the exponential manifestation of the seed sown. This is why you never sow an apple seed and reap one apple—you reap an entire apple tree. When you put this law into a spiritual context, it changes the way you see the world.

The Bible says, "*Be not deceived; God is not mocked: for whatsoever a man sows, that shall he also reap*" (Galatians 6:7). This is an irrevocable spiritual law. Just like all laws, it is meant to be respected. When you fail to respect a law, you will experience an adverse result. Many people experience scarcity in their lives because they violate the law of the seed. Imagine a farmer going to his field and expecting a harvest when he has planted no seed in the ground. What would you say to that farmer? You would probably tell him that he is delusional. Why, then, do we expect a spiritual harvest when we have sown no seed?

If you desire more faith, you must sow the seed of the Word into your heart. If you desire better relationships, you must sow the seed of trust. No matter what area of your life in which you desire to see a harvest, the key is planting the right seed. One day, my wife came to me and said, "Kynan, I believe the Lord wants you to sow your entire first paycheck to the Lord." Honestly, I thought she had gone mad. This was a very sacrificial request. Yet being the man of faith that I was, I obeyed the instruction. Several weeks later, someone gave us a car. Hallelujah. This is not about gimmicks and tricks; this is about faith in God's Word. Are you ready for the greatest harvest you have ever seen in your life? Allow the Holy Spirit to direct you as to which seed He would have you sow. Whatever He tells you to do, do it, and you will be blessed.

Day 64: BREAKTHROUGH PRAYER

Father, I know that You are the Lord of the harvest. You have said in Your Word that as long as the earth remains, there will be seedtime and harvest. I submit myself to the law of the seed. I declare that I have good seed in good ground, and I reap a vibrant harvest, in the name of Jesus. I speak crop failure to every bad seed that I have sown in my life or in the lives of others. Holy Spirit, speak to me regarding what You would have me do. I receive Your strategic direction about the way that will transform my life and destiny. I walk in supernatural obedience; therefore, I will walk in supernatural blessings all the days of my life. In Jesus's name, amen.

Day 65: No More Distractions

Turn not to the right hand nor to the left: remove your foot from evil. (Proverbs 4:27)

In my book *Kingdom Authority*, I talk about the four strategies the enemy of our souls uses against us. One of those strategies is distraction. A distraction is something that takes your attention away from what you should be focused on. There are many distractions in the world today, including television and the Internet, especially social media. The enemy's scheme is to create so much noise in your life that your attention is drawn away from God and what He has called and ordained you to do.

What if I told you that many of the challenges you face daily are simply distractions? They are designed to derail your faith and trust in God. I remember a time when God told me I was about to enter into the best season of my life to that point. The moment I received that word from God, it seemed like all hell broke loose. My finances, marriage, children, and ministry were all affected by the situation. Little did I know that this was all a smokescreen designed to take my attention away from the Most High. After some time, I realized that it was simply a distraction. When I came into this understanding, I took authority in Christ and began to worship God in spirit and in truth. Today, I have learned to see through the enemy's lies and smokescreens. I challenge you today to refuse to be distracted. Keep your eyes on the Prize!

Day 65: BREAKTHROUGH PRAYER

Father, thank You for who You are and all that You have done in my life. I declare that I am a new creation in Christ Jesus. I recognize that Your Word admonishes me not to go to the left or to the right but rather straight ahead in Your ways, and to stay away from evil. Hebrews 12:2 says that Jesus endured the cross because of the joy that was set before Him—the many rewards of His sacrifice. I declare that my eyes are open to see eternal rewards and blessings in the earth. In Jesus's name, amen.

Day 66: Birthing the Miraculous

And Stephen, full of faith and power, did great wonders and miracles among the people. (Acts 6:8)

The Bible says that signs and wonders will follow the believer. (See Mark 16:17.) Whether you know it or not, every single believer has been called to live a miraculous life. Your title or position in the church does not matter—God desires to express Himself through you. We are called to be "carriers" of the kingdom through the Spirit of God who dwells within us. If you are going to be a person who manifests supernatural breakthroughs in your life, you must embrace the biblical mandate to live as Jesus did, in the realm of the miraculous.

Remember that Jesus said, *"You shall know the truth, and the truth shall make you free"* (John 8:32). The word *"know"* here is more than head knowledge; it is knowledge that comes from relationship and interaction, and it can refer to intimacy. This is the same word in Hebrew used for intimacy between a husband and a wife that produces children. In other words, knowing the truth of God's Word must impregnate us and produce something. Contrary to popular belief, you don't receive miracles—you give birth to them. The Holy Spirit is the birthing coach of the Christian life. He is the One who stands alongside us and empowers us to release the supernatural.

A life of miracles is a life of power. The great healing evangelist Kathryn Kuhlman was noted for saying, "I believe in miracles." Do you believe in miracles? Don't be misled—miracles were not just for the patriarchs of the Bible; God's desire is for you to birth miracles today. Yet, as with most pregnancies, there may be birth pangs. Many people are frustrated because they know there is more potential inside them than what they are producing in their lives. I challenge you to "push" and birth the manifestation of God's promises. I challenge you to press through until something happens. Don't just settle for a mediocre or stagnant Christian life—there is so much more! Meditate on God's Word. Get His truth deep down inside you, and begin to place a claim on it by faith. Before you know it, your life will experience a miraculous shift. Are you ready for miracles to become an everyday part of your life? Stop asking God to send you a miracle. Start birthing them!

Day 66: BREAKTHROUGH PRAYER

Father, I believe in miracles. I know You are a miracle-working God. I know You have called me to live a supernatural lifestyle. Therefore, I declare that from this day forward, I give birth to the miraculous. Signs and wonders are a regular part of my everyday life. I release the kingdom of God according to Mark 16:17, through signs, wonders, and miracles. I know that signs and wonders are not an end in themselves but are a means of bringing glory to the name of Jesus Christ and His kingdom. Today, I step out by faith and do the impossible according to Your Word. I refuse to bow to fear; instead, I have bold confidence in the Word of God and move according to Your desire. Nothing is impossible to me because I am a believer in the Word of God and not a doubter. I give birth to the miraculous today, in Jesus's name! Amen.

Day 67: First-Class Citizen

For our conversation [citizenship, lifestyle] *is in heaven; from where also we look for the Savior, the Lord Jesus Christ.* (Philippians 3:20)

As I mentioned in a previous devotional, I am a *very* frequent flyer. However, I remember a particular flight to the United Kingdom that was my first time flying to Europe. It was also my first time flying first class. I sat in literally the first seat on the plane behind the cockpit. The flight attendant brought me juice, appetizers, and desserts throughout the flight. I never received this kind of treatment when I traveled in coach! Then it dawned on me: the way you were treated depended on where you were positioned. The closer you were to the captain of the plane, the better your flight experience.

That understanding gave me a revelation about the kingdom of God. Through the blood of Jesus, the Father has seated us in "first class" in the heavenly places. (See Ephesians 2:6.) On the airplane, a greater level of favor and access was given to those in first class than those who were not seated in first class. Why? Because of the *price* that was paid. God paid the ultimate price to make us first-class citizens in heaven: He offered up His only begotten Son. Yet, if God paid such a price to see us in first class, why do many of us behave like we are still in coach?

You are not a second-class citizen! You are a citizen of the kingdom of God. The favor of God is upon your life. You are not ordinary or average—you are extraordinary. The key to understanding this truth is revelation knowledge. The Bible says that God's people *"are destroyed for lack of knowledge"* (Hosea 4:6). Many Christians still don't know their position and identity in Christ. They don't comprehend the price their heavenly Father paid to change their status—or the riches Christ has won for them. As a result of this ignorance, they allow the enemy to buffet them unnecessarily. The devil is a liar. The reality is that you are *"the head, and not the tail."* You are above and not beneath. (See Deuteronomy 28:13.) The Father has given you *"all things to enjoy"* (1 Timothy 6:17), and now is the time for you to enjoy them. Stop allowing the enemy to lie to you and tell you that you are nothing, that you will always be a "wretched sinner." You are no longer trapped in sin. You are the righteousness of God in Christ Jesus. (See 2 Corinthians 5:21.) The moment you receive these truths is the moment you will begin to enjoy a greater quality of life—spiritually, mentally, physically, and emotionally. You are traveling in first class. Now, act like it, and receive the blessings God offers you!

Day 67: BREAKTHROUGH PRAYER

> Father, I recognize that through the blood of Jesus Christ, I have been made a first-class citizen of Your kingdom. You have adopted me as Your child, and I am *"accepted in the beloved."* Therefore, I declare that "no evil will befall my dwelling." I will no longer settle for a lower level of living. Today, my level has changed. I choose to live on the level of revelation. Thank You for Your supernatural favor in my life. I am more than a conqueror through Jesus who loves me. I declare that miraculous doors open for me because of my identity

in Christ. I will no longer live like a pauper; I recognize that I am a King's kid and will live accordingly. Thank You, Lord, for the supernatural power of God working in my life. In Jesus's name, amen. (See Ephesians 1:6; Psalm 91:10; Romans 8:37.)

Day 68: Money Miracles

A feast is made for laughter, and wine makes merry: but money answers all things. (Ecclesiastes 10:19)

The first time I ever really saw a money miracle was in Israel several years ago. A friend of mine was praying for miracles to take place in people's finances. Minutes later, my wife sent me a text message that we had just received twenty thousand dollars. Wow! Talk about the supernatural! Since that time, I have seen and experienced hundreds, if not thousands, of money miracles. On another occasion, a woman in our church walked up and handed us a check for over twenty thousand dollars. This was not a response to any request or fund-raising campaign; it was unexpected, supernatural provision. I believe that God is about to manifest supernatural miracles in the area of finances for many people in the body of Christ. These miracles are not for our benefit alone but to advance the kingdom of God.

Contrary to popular belief, money miracles are very common in the Bible. For example, when taxes were due, Jesus told Peter, "*Notwithstanding, lest we should offend them, go you to the sea, and cast a hook, and take up the fish that first comes up; and when you have opened its mouth, you shall find a piece of money: that take, and give to them for Me and you*" (Matthew 17:27). Peter found money in the mouth of a fish when he obeyed the instructions of Jesus. What would happen if you and I obeyed the instructions of Jesus—no matter how foolish they might seem to us? What if I told you that your breakthrough was one act of obedience away? I believe that the miracle you are looking for is in your obedience. As I mentioned previously, I have seen debts canceled, finances turned around, and hidden money discovered by the power of the Holy Spirit.

One young man was preaching in an evening meeting, and a businessman walked in, wrote out a check for one million dollars, left it for him, and walked out again. That's what you call a money miracle! God does not show partiality. If He can abundantly provide for one of us, He can do it for all of us. Are you ready to receive your miracle? The key is faith and obedience. *"If you be willing and obedient, you shall eat the good of the land"* (Isaiah 1:19). Receive your miracle today!

Day 68: BREAKTHROUGH PRAYER

Father, You are the God of miracles. Just as You manifested miraculous financial miracles in the Bible, I am believing that You will manifest a financial miracle in my life today. The Word declares that wealth and riches will be in my house; therefore, I declare that everything You have promised is attracted to me. I declare that the curse of poverty is broken off of my life. Instead, "the blessing of the Lord that makes rich and adds no sorrow" is upon me. Thank You that I am free of debt, in the name of Jesus. I have more than enough to be a blessing to the kingdom of God. My hands will give to the poor and the needy. Today is my day for miracles. In Jesus's name, amen! (See Psalm 112:1, 3; Proverbs 10:22; Proverbs 19:17.)

Day 69: Seated in Heavenly Places

[God] *has raised us up together, and made us sit together in heavenly places in Christ Jesus.* (Ephesians 2:6)

The first time I went to a large wedding in Africa, I realized the importance of seating arrangements. In African culture, just like many other cultures, where you are seated at a wedding says a lot about who you are. The most esteemed guests sit at the very front. Those who are part of the bridal party sit at the head table. This is one of the easiest ways to identify who is who. Likewise, being a Master of seating arrangements, God has seated us together with Christ Jesus in the heavenly places. What does that mean, exactly? It means that we are part of the royal family. That's right! We are no longer outsiders. Through the blood of Jesus Christ, we have become "*heirs of God, and joint-heirs with Christ*" (Romans 8:17). This fact is absolutely amazing.

Again, "religion" may have taught you that you are "just a wretched sinner saved by grace," but nothing could be further from the truth. You are a part of the family of God, significant in Him. I want to reemphasize the fact that religion has sold us a lie. We have been taught that we are nothing. We have been taught that we have no value. We have been taught that we are worthless. But that is not the case for the redeemed in Christ. Not only are we seated together with Him in heavenly places, but we are also exalted far above all principalities and powers. (See Ephesians 1:20–21.) No demon in hell is invited to this table. Why, then, do we entertain the lies of the enemy? He doesn't want us to know where we're seated. He wants us to believe that we are something other than what God says we are. But if we will simply grab hold of this truth by faith, our lives will never be the same.

God is calling you into a radical experience with His Spirit. This radical experience begins with an understanding of your true identity. When you realize you are a son or daughter of the Most High God, the spirit of vain tradition or religion will lose its power over you. It's time to change the way you think. It's time to think like a King's kid!

Day 69: BREAKTHROUGH PRAYER

Father, I thank You that I am a child of the King. I have been seated together with Jesus in heavenly places. In Christ, You have exalted me far above all principalities of darkness that would oppress or attack me. I declare that I am part of a "*chosen generation*" and a "*royal priesthood.*" You called me out of darkness and into Your marvelous light. As a citizen of the kingdom of God, I exercise my rights of victorious living. I am more than a conqueror because You love me. I refuse to accept defeat as my portion. I declare that I am empowered to walk in my kingdom identity. I will never be a victim of fear, defeat, regret, depression, or despair. Power and grace are flowing in and through my life, to the glory of God. I declare that You are the lifter of my head. In Jesus's name, amen. (See 1 Peter 2:9; Romans 8:37; Psalm 3:3.)

Day 70: The Sound of Breakthrough

> *And suddenly there came a sound from heaven as of a rushing mighty wind, and it filled all the house where they were sitting.* (Acts 2:2)

In the beginning, God *spoke* the earth into being. In fact, the entire natural universe was created by His words. For example, He said, "*Let there be light: and there was light*" (Genesis 1:3). Furthermore, everything in the kingdom of God moves according to sound. What do I mean by this? Spoken words are comprised of sound. This is why the Bible says that "*faith comes by hearing, and hearing by the word of God*" (Romans 10:17). Accordingly, there is a sound of breakthrough. The "sound" you make creates the atmosphere for the miracle you will receive.

Let me give you a biblical illustration of this. "*And, behold, two blind men sitting by the way side, when they heard that Jesus passed by, cried out, saying, Have mercy on us, O Lord,* [O] *Son of David*" (Matthew 20:30). These two blind men cried out to the Lord. Their desperation motivated a powerful cry from the depths of their souls, and it caused Jesus to stand still and call them to Him. (See verse 32.) Their gut-level cry became the catalyst for the miracle for which they were believing, and they received their sight. Their call brought a response from heaven.

Similarly, the sound you release creates the atmosphere for breakthrough, which prompts a supernatural response from heaven. I want you to imagine military fighter jets flying through the sky. Such jets fly so fast they break the sound barrier. You often can't see them, but you can hear them because of the sonic boom they create. I believe that you are about to experience a sonic boom in the realm of the Spirit—a manifestation of the explosive power of God working in your life to bring about change and transformation. The disciples heard the sound of heaven *"as of a rushing mighty wind"* in the upper room when the Holy Spirit broke through the stratosphere and entered the earthly realm. This sound was the evidence that everything had changed—for their lives and for the world. I don't know what you are experiencing today, but I hear the sound of the abundance of rain flowing in your life. (See 1 Kings 17:41.) It doesn't matter what things look like in the natural—*"faith comes by hearing, and hearing by the word of God."* Open your mouth and declare breakthrough. Release the Word of God, and witness the manifestation of His mighty power in your life. Something is moving, something is changing—heaven is invading the earth!

Day 70: BREAKTHROUGH PRAYER

Father, I hear the sound of the abundance of rain flowing in my life. I hear the sound of breakthrough emanating from the courts of heaven. I declare that my change has come. I declare breakthrough in every area of my life. I declare that miracles are happening right now. I release a sound of revival and awakening from my mouth that affects the atmosphere around me, impregnating it for miracles. I recognize that something supernatural is taking place. Whether I can see it with my natural eyes or not, I hear the sound of it. I declare that miracles are my portion. Thank You, God, that my life will never be the same again. In Jesus's name, amen.

Day 71: The Manifold Grace of God

As every man has received the gift, even so minister the same one to another, as good stewards of the manifold grace of God. (1 Peter 4:10)

The Lord spoke to me some time ago and told me that this would be a season of the manifold grace of God. The Bible says that we are to be *"good stewards of the manifold grace of God."* What is the *"manifold grace of God,"* and how are we to be good stewards of it? The manifold grace simply means the multifaceted grace of God. In other words, grace has many dimensions. The Bible talks about grace in many ways, such as the favor of God, the goodness of God, the power of God, and the influence of God. And there are many kinds of grace that affect us in varying situations. We experienced the grace of salvation when we were born again. We experience grace when we receive healing in our bodies. We experience grace when we have a financial breakthrough. We experience grace when the Holy Spirit grants us repentance from an area of sin or iniquity in our lives. We receive grace to minister the gifts of the Spirit. We access God's grace to be loving spouses and parents, and to live the Christian life every day. All of this and more is available to us if we will simply believe it and receive it.

The Bible says, *"The law was given by Moses, but grace and truth came by Jesus Christ"* (John 1:17), and *"By grace are you saved through faith; and that not of yourselves: it is the gift of God"* (Ephesians 2:8). Grace is a gift. You cannot earn a gift; you can only receive it. But once that gift is received, it must be handled properly. Many people are poor stewards of the grace of God. As noted earlier, some people consider grace as a license to do whatever they want to do rather than an empowerment to do what God calls us to do. Beloved, that is not your portion. I believe you are about to experience the grace of God in measures you cannot even dare to ask, think, or imagine. (See Ephesians 3:20.) God is about to show you just how good He really is. What if I told you that the days of the greatest manifestation of the grace of God are before you? Well, they are! Get ready to receive the manifold grace of God today.

Day 71: BREAKTHROUGH PRAYER

Father, Your Word declares, *"For by grace are you saved through faith; and that not of yourselves: it is the gift of God: not of works, lest any man should boast."* As an act of my faith, I receive Your supernatural grace and favor. I declare that Your grace empowers me to live victoriously. I declare that Your goodness fills my life. I declare that Your grace instructs me to deny ungodliness and to live above the shackles of sin and shame. I declare that Your grace enables me to experience Your divine favor in every area of my life. I declare that I am walking in the accelerated manifestation of every promise You have ever made to me in Your Word. Nothing will stand in the way of my destiny in You. In the name of Jesus, amen. (See Ephesians 2:8–9; Titus 2:12.)

Day 72: Kingdom Culture

But seek you first the kingdom of God, and His righteousness; and all these things shall be added to you.

(Matthew 6:33)

One of the most frustrating experiences a person can have is to be in a new place or in a different country and not understand the culture and customs there. The first time I went to Africa, I was blown away by some of the varying cultural expressions I witnessed and experienced, which were much different from my own. For example, I will never forget the first time I walked into a room and people began to bow. I was so uncomfortable I didn't know what to do. Apparently, this was their custom.

Culture can be defined as "the ideas, customs, and social behavior of a particular people or society," or "the attitudes and behavior characteristic of a particular social group." Just as the earthly realm has various cultures, the kingdom of God has a culture. And the key to living a successful Christian life is understanding and embracing the culture of God's kingdom. Jesus said, "*Seek you first the kingdom of God, and His righteousness; and all these things shall be added to you.*" In other words, He was telling us to seek the culture of God's kingdom—His influence and His right way of doing things—and everything we need will be given to us. Most people neglect this Scripture. Instead, they seek the "things" first and put the kingdom last. Nothing will cause more frustration in your life then doing something contrary to God's Word.

What is the culture of the kingdom? Faith, love, and obedience. When it comes to God, we *"must believe that He is, and that He is a rewarder of them that diligently seek Him"* (Hebrews 11:6). To live in the culture of the kingdom is to love God and keep His commandments. If we would learn to embrace the simple truths of kingdom culture, instilling this culture into our lives, we would see a greater manifestation of the supernatural.

Day 72: BREAKTHROUGH PRAYER

Father, thank You for Your kingdom and Your righteousness. I declare that Your kingdom is my priority. You said in Your Word that the kingdom of God is within me. I live according to the influence of the Word of God. As Your Word permeates my heart, I walk in perfect obedience to Your truth. I submit myself to Your way of doing things. May everyone around me see who You are by my attitudes, behavior, and actions. The Word declares that *"God is love"*; therefore, I walk in Your agape love. I daily live according to Your precepts. My deepest desire is to do what is pleasing in Your sight. I release the culture of the kingdom into the earth by faith. In Jesus's name, amen. (See Luke 17:21; 1 John 4:8, 16; 1 John 3:22.)

Day 73: The Ministry of the Holy Spirit

But the Comforter, which is the Holy Ghost, whom the Father will send in My name, He shall teach you all things, and bring all things to your remembrance, whatsoever I have said to you. (John 14:26)

I remember the year I received the baptism of the Holy Spirit. It was 1996, and as I sat on my couch watching a minister on Christian television, I said a prayer to be filled with the Spirit. When I received the baptism of the Holy Spirit, I immediately knew that my life had changed forever. I was able to hear from God more clearly. I began to receive words of knowledge about people and situations. And there was a level of peace in my soul that I could not explain.

Unfortunately, many people are ignorant of the present ministry of the Holy Spirit at work on earth today. As Dr. Myles Munroe would say, He is the most important Person on earth. "*You shall receive power, after that the Holy Ghost is come upon you*" (Acts 1:8). The power of the Holy Spirit enables us to live effective Christian lives. What good is making it to heaven if you can't take anybody with you? Many Christians have a fruitless witness because they neglect the Holy Spirit's presence in their lives. He is the agent of revival in the earth. He is the One who leads us into all truth. He is the One who anoints and empowers us for Christian service. He is the One who enables us to release the kingdom of God in the earth.

The Bible says, "*God anointed Jesus of Nazareth with the Holy Ghost and with power: who went about doing good, and healing all that were oppressed of the devil*" (Acts 10:38). The secret to miracles is intimacy with the Holy Spirit. He is the power source of the supernatural. Unless we submit to and engage the Holy Spirit, we cannot live the kind of life the Bible talks about. However, when we learn to be intimate with, and obedient to, the Holy Spirit, we will experience the explosive power of God in our lives. I challenge you with this today: Get to know the Holy Spirit. Ask God to anoint you afresh with His power. Holy Spirit, You are welcome; have Your way in us!

Day 73: BREAKTHROUGH PRAYER

Father, thank You for the gift of Your Holy Spirit. Through Your Spirit, I am empowered to live a miraculous life. Through Your Spirit, I receive downloads from heaven that grant me supernatural insight into Your will and purpose for my life. Father, You said in Your Word that we would receive power after the Holy Spirit comes upon us; therefore, I declare that I walk in Your power every day. By Your Spirit, I will heal the sick, I will raise the dead, and I will cast out demons. Lord, Your Word says that the Holy Spirit will bring all things to our remembrance that Jesus has taught us; therefore, I declare that I have divine recovery of every instruction, insight, and strategy of God for my life. Holy Spirit, I grant You full permission to lead and guide me as You desire. I ask You to flow in my life today and every day. In Jesus's name, amen. (See John 14:26.)

Day 74: Freedom from Discouragement

And David was greatly distressed; for the people spoke of stoning him, because the soul of all the people was grieved, every man for his sons and for his daughters: but David encouraged himself in the Lord *his God.*

(1 Samuel 30:6)

Have you ever been discouraged? Haven't we all? Discouragement is defined as "a loss of confidence or enthusiasm." Discouragement can make a person feel that God is not with them. It was the psalmist David who wrote, "*Restore to me the joy of Your salvation*" (Psalm 51:12). Do you need your joy restored today? David understood what it means to face discouragement. One time, due to an overwhelming incident that we discussed in an earlier devotional, he was so distressed by loss that he was ready to give up. But remember that David "*encouraged himself in the* Lord *his God.*"

What is more powerful than discouragement? It is encouragement. If you are facing distress, discouragement, or despair, the God of the universe is calling you today to encourage yourself in Him. How can you do this? The Bible says, "*They* [the saints] *overcame him* [the devil] *by the blood of the Lamb, and by the word of their testimony*" (Revelation 12:11). Encourage yourself by your own testimonies of God's faithfulness. Remind yourself of the goodness He has demonstrated throughout your life. Remind yourself of each time God has healed you, delivered you, or brought you out of a difficult situation. Talk to your soul. In Psalms, David talked to his soul, saying, "*Why are you cast down, O my soul? and why are you disquieted within me? hope in God: for I shall yet praise Him, who is the health of my countenance, and my God*" (Psalm 43:5; see also Psalm 42:5, 11). Tell your soul to come out of the pit of despair. Begin to recite all of the powerful and wonderful acts of God in your life. Speak the Word over yourself. Pray in the Spirit. I declare that you are free from the spirit of discouragement. "*Why are you cast down, O my soul? and why are you disquieted within me? hope in God.*"

Day 74: BREAKTHROUGH PRAYER

Father, in the name of Jesus, I thank You for who You are and all that You have done in my life. I declare that my soul is lifted up in You. I declare that I am free from discouragement. I declare that no weapon formed against me will be able to prosper, and that any tongue that rises against me in judgment will be condemned. I declare that depression no longer has power over me. Shackles of despondency are broken off of my life. I declare that greater is He that is in me than he that is in the world. Today, I experience a supernatural revival and renewal of joy in my life. In the name of Jesus, amen. (See Isaiah 54:17; 1 John 4:4.)

Day 75: Recognize and Release

Blessed be the God and Father of our Lord Jesus Christ, who has blessed us with all spiritual blessings in heavenly places in Christ. (Ephesians 1:3)

What if I told you that everything God was going to bless you with, He has already blessed you with? What if I told you that everything you are asking God for has already been given to you? Well, that is exactly what the Bible says. The Word of God affirms that we have been blessed *"with all spiritual blessings in heavenly places in Christ."* In other words, everything that we need has already been given to us. It is finished. What should we do in order to enjoy these blessings? We just need to recognize and release them.

Jesus said that whatever we bind on earth will be bound in heaven, and whatever we loose on earth will be loosed in heaven. (See Matthew 16:19; 18:18.) The word *loose* simply means to untie, unfasten, or release. Whatever we release from the earth is released from heaven. This means that in order to receive something from God, we must place a claim, or a demand, upon it. Let me explain a little more what I mean by a "demand." Demanding is not an act of arrogance but rather an act of acknowledgment. Simply put, you must recognize what belongs to you and decide if you are ready to receive it. Think of it like an inheritance. If a child has been designated as heir in their parents' last will and testament, but they never place a claim on their inheritance or receive what they are offered, they will never benefit from it. Jesus paid the ultimate price to give us an inheritance from our heavenly Father—His own life. Yet millions of Christians all over the world are not enjoying the life that He paid for. Today, I want to challenge you to recognize what the Father has given you and release it by faith, in Jesus's name.

Day 75: BREAKTHROUGH PRAYER

Father, I recognize that You are the Lord of all the earth. You said in Your Word that You have "*blessed us with all spiritual blessings in heavenly places in Christ.*" I declare that I am a child of the Most High God; therefore, I receive my inheritance by faith. I recognize and release everything You have graciously prepared for me. I declare that Your will for my life is good, and that, accordingly, I will live a good life and see good days. I declare that I will live to see "*the goodness of the Lord in the land of the living.*" I declare that I will "*not die, but live, and declare the works of the Lord.*" I declare that the fulfillment of every promise that has been held up in the spiritual realm is released right now. I declare that every spiritual blessing that You have given me in the heavenly realms is mine to possess. Thank You for all of Your blessings in my life. In Jesus's name, amen. (See Psalm 34:12–15; 1 Peter 3:10–12; Psalm 27:13; Psalm 118:17.)

Day 76: Release the Increase

Hear therefore, O Israel, and observe to do it; that it may be well with you, and that you may increase mightily as the LORD *God of your fathers has promised you, in the land that flows with milk and honey.* (Deuteronomy 6:3)

One of the things I am constantly reminded of in Scripture is that God is a God of increase. The Bible teaches that we were created to *"be fruitful, and multiply"* (Genesis 1:22, 28). Thus, at the very beginning, at creation, God spoke the language of increase. Everything that God created was programmed to increase. In fact, if we are not experiencing increase in our lives, we are not operating according to the pattern and plan of God. As much as people might try to explain this truth away, deficiency and lack are not in God's vocabulary. He is incapable of barrenness.

In Deuteronomy 28, God promised the Israelites that they would experience increase in various areas of their lives. I don't know about you, but I want to experience the land flowing with milk and honey! This is simply another way of explaining that God's will is for His people to prosper. That's right, I said it again: prosperity. The word *prosperity* is not profanity. God desires for us to prosper in every area of our lives. He wants us to be complete and whole, with nothing missing, nothing broken. This is what the word *shālēm,* a Hebrew term for "restore," is all about.

How do we experience this biblical prosperity? How do we release the increase? Once more, the key is obedience. "If we are willing and obedient, we will eat the good of the land." (See Isaiah 1:19.) Nothing positions us to enjoy the blessings of God like obedience. I can attest to the fact that disobedience will stagnate your blessings. I was guilty of walking in disobedience for many years, and I was very frustrated by the lack and emptiness it caused. One day, God spoke to me, asking me a very simple question: "Kynan, have you done what I've asked you to do?" I had to confess my disobedience to the Lord. The truth was, I had not been living according to His perfect will for my life. I am not referring to having committed a "major" sin, but simply disobeying His instructions. The moment I obeyed was the moment I saw the accelerated manifestation of His increase in my life. Are you ready to release the increase? I challenge you to obey God's Word today and see His miraculous hand working in your life.

Day 76: BREAKTHROUGH PRAYER

Father, thank You for Your greatness and all the blessings You give us. I declare that I walk in kingdom abundance. By faith, I release increase in my life. I obey Your Word daily. As I walk in obedience, I anticipate great favor and blessings upon my life, in Jesus's name. Father, You said in Your Word that You would not withhold any good thing from those who "*walk uprightly*"; therefore, I declare that I walk uprightly according to Your will. I declare that I go "*from faith to faith*" and "*from glory to glory.*" I declare that, this time next year, I will have received increase that is a thousand times greater than what I have today. Thank You for blessing me and enlarging my territory. In Jesus's name, amen. (See Psalm 84:11; Romans 1:17; 2 Corinthians 3:18; 1 Chronicles 4:10 NIV.)

Day 77: Praise Your Way Through

And at midnight Paul and Silas prayed, and sang praises to God: and the prisoners heard them. And suddenly there was a great earthquake, so that the foundations of the prison were shaken: and immediately all the doors were opened, and every one's bands were loosed.

(Acts 16:25–26)

Years ago, I was talking to a mentor of mine, and he challenged me in a way I had never been challenged up to that point. He said to me, "Kynan, stop trying to pray your way into the presence of God, and start praising your way into the presence of God." Honestly, at the time, I didn't understand what he was talking about. But several months later, I began to comprehend what the Lord was trying to tell me. You see, I had focused much of my energy struggling to pray, often with no breakthrough. Have you ever had seasons when your prayer life was dry? That was exactly how I felt until the Lord gave me this revelation. As I began to implement praise in the manner in which my mentor had instructed me, I saw a drastic shift in the way I encountered God's presence. These words resonated in my spirit: "Praise your way through."

Whatever situation you face today, you need to learn to use praise as a weapon of spiritual warfare. Your praise is like the battering ram of the Spirit. Paul and Silas understood this concept very well. When they were trapped in prison with nowhere to go, they employed the power of praise. They praised their way through the captivity. The Bible records that as they praised and sang, the Holy Spirit invaded the room. Their bands were loosed and the prison cells were opened. (See Act 16:12–33.) What if I told you that praise could break you out of any situation that you're in? If we would simply learn to praise our way through—not complaining or worrying but praising the name of the Lord—we would experience breakthrough. Praise is simply recognizing and acknowledging who God is and what He is able to do. We need to thank God for what He has already done in our lives.

God is more than able to deliver you out of any situation you face. If you are battling sickness and disease, praise your way through it. If you are stuck in a rut, praise your way through it. If you are in debt, praise your way through it. No matter what the difficulty, praise is the battering ram that will break you out.

Day 77: BREAKTHROUGH PRAYER

Father, I thank You for who You are and all that You have done in my life. I declare that praise is one of my weapons of spiritual warfare, and I use this weapon to break out of any situation that would hold me in captivity. Just as Paul and Silas prayed and sang praises, and the Holy Spirit broke them out of prison, I declare that as I pray and praise, the power of the Holy Spirit will be released and break all shackles of bondage off my life. My worship is "my warship." I will use the weapon of praise and demolish the strongholds of the enemy, right now, in the name of Jesus. Amen.

Day 78: The Power of Thanksgiving

Rooted and built up in Him, and established in the faith, as you have been taught, abounding therein with thanksgiving. (Colossians 2:7)

Almost nothing in this earth is more contagious or all-inspiring than gratitude. Do you have an attitude of gratitude? You may have heard the saying, "Your attitude will determine your altitude," and that is so true. How high you go in the kingdom of God is often connected with the level of thanksgiving in your heart. This is what I call the "law of thanksgiving." The Bible says that we should make our prayers, supplications, and requests with thanksgiving. (See Philippians 4:6.) In other words, once you have asked God for something, begin to thank Him for what you have asked Him, as if you have already received it.

So again, I ask: Do you have an attitude of gratitude? How much would your life change if you embraced an attitude of thanksgiving every single day? Stop complaining about the things you don't have. Stop comparing yourself to others. Stop rehearsing the past or negative situations you have experienced. Doing these things will only cause stagnation in your life. If you opt for an attitude of gratitude, you will begin to see an accelerated manifestation of God's blessings and promises in your life.

Have you ever done something for someone, and they were extremely ungrateful? How did it make you feel? Probably more reluctant to do the same thing for them again. It works the same way spiritually. God wants us to be in relationship with Him, not just to take from Him. The more thankful we are, the more we will walk in the blessings of God. The more ungrateful we are, the more we will miss the blessings of God for our lives. I don't know about you, but I choose to be grateful because God has been extremely good to me. If I had ten thousand tongues, I couldn't thank Him enough for what He has done in my life. Today, let us give thanks to the Lord with a grateful heart, because He deserves it.

Day 78: BREAKTHROUGH PRAYER

Father, in the name of Jesus, I thank You for all that You are and all that You have done in my life. I am grateful for the love and grace You have shown toward me. I refuse to complain about the situations and circumstances of my life. I refuse to be bitter or angry over any negative thing I have experienced. You have shown me much goodness, and I will not compare myself to anyone else. I declare that I possess a grateful heart. I declare that I have an attitude of gratitude. I declare that my attitude of gratitude increases my altitude, in Jesus's name. I declare that negativity, worry, and anxiety have no place in my heart and mind. I declare that Your favor surrounds me like a shield. I give thanks to You with a grateful heart, and I position myself to receive supernatural blessings in my life. Thank You, Lord, for Your great grace and goodness to me. In Jesus's name, amen. (See Psalm 5:12.)

Day 79: The Law of Cheerfulness

Every man according as he purposed in his heart, so let him give; not grudgingly, or of necessity: for God loves a cheerful giver. (2 Corinthians 9:7)

Did you know that "*God loves a cheerful giver*"? Not a fearful giver, or a tearful giver, but a cheerful giver. I'm sure you have heard the above Scripture quoted many times at church when an offering was about to be collected. But what if I told you that this Scripture unlocks a secret to kingdom abundance? This, my friend, is "the law of cheerfulness."

What exactly is the law of cheerfulness? I'm glad you asked. The word "*cheerful*" in this verse is derived from a Greek word that literally means "hilarious." Paul the apostle was admonishing the church to give "hilariously." The Bible says, "*A merry heart does good like a medicine*" (Proverbs 17:22). To give cheerfully is to give with an attitude of happiness and optimism. Taking this further, cheerfulness implies that we are so excited about giving that we are literally laughing. The Scriptures encourage us that "*the joy of the Lord is* [our] *strength*" (Nehemiah 8:10). Have you ever heard someone laugh with such joy and vigor that you started laughing as well? Just as laughter is contagious, cheerfulness is contagious.

When we give cheerfully and live cheerfully, we are dwelling in hope and expectation. And the attitude of expectancy is the atmosphere for miracles. I challenge you today to laugh at the schemes of the devil. He thought that by attacking you, he could stop you, but he has another thing coming. Laugh at the enemy's machinations because he is a liar, and he is already defeated. As you go about your day today, be cheerful in everything you do. Live hilariously!

Day 79: BREAKTHROUGH PRAYER

Father, I give thanks with a grateful heart because You are good and Your mercy endures forever. The law of cheerfulness requires that I be optimistic and have confidence in Your Word. Therefore, I anticipate good things happening in my life, and I prophecy that everyone who comes near me will experience the joy of the Lord. I position myself to receive miracles. I declare that the joy of the Lord is my strength. I am happy because You have been so good to me all the days of my life. I refuse to be cynical and negative about anything because You have given me every reason to praise You with all of my heart. I give thanks with a cheerful heart because You are my banner, my strength, and my righteousness. I declare that my cheerfulness is contagious, and my life is filled with new joy. In Jesus's name, amen. (See Psalm 100:5; 106:1; 118:29.)

Day 80: Simply Believe

Therefore I say to you, What things soever you desire, when you pray, believe that you receive them, and you shall have them. (Mark 11:24)

Everything in the Christian life is centered on our faith and trust in God. Simply put, what we believe will determine how we live and what we experience. The Bible says, *"Faith is the substance of things hoped for, the evidence of things not seen"* (Hebrews 11:1). Do you believe the Word of God? Jesus told Martha that if she would believe, she would see the glory of God. (See John 11:40.) To believe simply means to accept something as true. Many people today have never seen their birth certificates, yet they believe that their names are what their parents told them they are. My children have never seen their birth certificates, but they respond to what I call them. Why? Because they believe.

Likewise, when we believe what God says, we accept the truth of His Word as our reality. David said that he would have fainted if he had not believed he would see *"the goodness of the Lord in the land of the living"* (Psalm 27:13). You must believe in God and what He has said. It's that simple. Remember that *"Abraham believed God, and it was counted to him for righteousness"* (Romans 4:3; see also Genesis 15:6; Galatians 3:6; James 2:23). Abraham simply accepted what God said as the truth. This is what it means to believe.

What do you believe today? Do you believe that you are already healed? Do you believe that you already prosper? Do you believe that you have been made whole by the power of the blood of Jesus? Right believing translates to right living. This is why the enemy of your soul is constantly fighting against your capacity to believe. And this is why you must continually meditate on the Word of God. *"Faith comes by hearing, and hearing by the word of God"* (Romans 10:17). What you hear on a consistent basis affects what you believe. God is looking for a generation of people who will simply possess childlike faith and take Him at His word. The confession of your faith should be, "Father, if You said it, I believe it, and that settles it, in Jesus's name."

Day 80: BREAKTHROUGH PRAYER

Father, in the name of Jesus, I thank You for the power of Your Word. I believe that Your Word is true. I believe in miracles. I believe that I am more than a conqueror through Jesus who loves me. I believe that I have already overcome the enemy by the blood of the Lamb and by the word of my testimony. I declare that I have bold faith and confidence in Your Word. I accept Your Word as the absolute truth and the final authority in my life. *"All things work together for good to them that love God, to them who are the called according to His purpose"*; therefore, I declare that all things are working together for my good and for the glory of God. I declare that Your grace is working in my life. You said that if I would confess Jesus with my mouth and believe in my heart that You raised Him from the dead, I would be saved. I believe in my heart and declare with my mouth that every promise in Your Word belongs to me. In Jesus's name, amen. (See Romans 8:37; Revelation 12:11; Romans 8:28; Romans 10:9.)

Day 81: Overcoming Despair

Nay, in all these things we are more than conquerors through Him that loved us. (Romans 8:37)

We sometimes experience seasons in our lives when we feel overwhelmed by the circumstances around us. In these times, it is extremely important that we possess the right attitude. Possessing a negative outlook—especially one of despair—can be detrimental to our life and destiny. Despair is defined as "the complete loss or absence of hope." It was Solomon who wrote that "*hope deferred makes the heart sick*" (Proverbs 13:12). Many people are experiencing despair as the result of disappointments in their lives. Maybe they were waiting for God to do something for them, but they never saw it happen. Maybe they are, even now, believing God for healing in their body and it has yet to manifest. If we are not careful, our "hope deferred" can cause despair.

The apostle Paul was no stranger to despair. He wrote to the Corinthians that there was a time when he "*despaired even of life*" (2 Corinthians 1:8). Apparently, the circumstances were so bad he felt like giving up. If you were to go through half of the things that Paul went through, you would probably feel the same way. Yet, even in the midst of all such things, "*we are more than conquerors,*" as Paul also expressed. What does it mean for us to be more than conquerors? Simply put, we face a defeated foe. Jesus has overcome every situation and circumstance that may be causing us despair. He has already defeated depression.

He has already defeated fear. He has already defeated anxiety. These things are powerless in the face of the glorious victory of Jesus Christ on the cross. Therefore, rise up out of the pit of despair and take your place as a citizen of the kingdom of God. Tell depression that it no longer has power over you, in the name of Jesus. Tell fear that it is time for it to go. Let all negative feelings and attitudes know that you are walking in supernatural strength and victory today.

Day 81: BREAKTHROUGH PRAYER

> Father, thank You that You have delivered me from the shackles of despair. Today, the spirit of shame and bondage are broken off of my life. I will never again be a slave to fear, regret, or anxiety. No weapon formed against me will prosper; therefore, I declare that the weapons of despair and darkness are broken, in Jesus's name. I refuse to be depressed. I refuse to be afraid. I refuse to be in despair. I declare that I am more than a conqueror through Christ who loves me. In the name of Jesus, amen! (See Isaiah 54:17.)

Day 82: The Miraculous Turnaround

But Jesus turned Him about, and when He saw her, He said, Daughter, be of good comfort; your faith has made you whole. And the woman was made whole from that hour.
(Matthew 9:22)

Are you ready for a miraculous turnaround in your life? Are you ready for God to do something so remarkable that you can't explain it with words? Are you ready for your mind to be blown? In an earlier devotional, we discussed the story of the woman with the issue of blood, from the gospel of Luke. Here, we look at the same story from the perspective of Matthew's gospel. After the woman had touched the hem of Jesus's garment and been healed, *"Jesus turned Him about, and when He saw her, He said, Daughter, be of good comfort; your faith has made you whole."*

The original Greek word translated *"turned Him about"* means, among other things, "to bring back." This emphasizes to me the way in which the woman experienced supernatural restoration. Her faith caused Jesus to turn, and that was a prophetic representation of the work of God in her life. As Jesus turned, her situation was turned around. She was brought back to God's original design for her life. So I ask again: Are you ready for a miraculous turnaround in your own life? As I have expressed before, one of the enemy's biggest fears is that we will put our complete faith in God, expecting and anticipating that He will meet our needs.

The woman with the issue of blood said to herself, *"If I may but touch His* [Jesus's] *garment, I shall be whole"* (Matthew 9:21). What have you said to yourself today? What are you anticipating God to do in your life? Your expectation will determine your manifestation. God is in the turnaround business. He loves to take broken dreams and broken things and make them into masterpieces; we must simply believe. The woman with the issue of blood was in a seemingly hopeless situation, yet her faith produced a miraculous turnaround. Beloved, there is hope for you today. Your situation can turn around for the glory of God. Release your faith for supernatural breakthrough. Doors are opening for you right now—get in position to receive your miracle!

Day 82: BREAKTHROUGH PRAYER

Father, I thank You for Your mighty power working in my life. Today, I declare that I am ready for a miraculous turnaround. I declare that healing and deliverance are my portion. I release my faith in the Word of God, and I am living in expectation of a miracle. I will not let fear, discouragement, or disappointment stand in the way of my blessing. Instead, I stand in faith on the promises of God. Like the woman with the issue of blood, I declare within myself that I am touching Your Word, believing its promises and receiving my miracle. I declare that I will testify of the goodness of God in my life. I declare that Your supernatural power is working in and through me, transforming and conforming me to the image of Jesus. I declare that whatever is broken in my life will become a masterpiece, according to Your sovereign design. In Jesus's name, amen.

Day 83: The Spirit of Revival

Though I walk in the midst of trouble, You will revive me: You shall stretch forth Your hand against the wrath of my enemies, and Your right hand shall save me.

(Psalm 138:7)

As I've previously stated, I believe we are about to experience the greatest revival in human history. I make such a bold claim because the Word of God says that the glory of the "*latter house*" will be greater than the "*former.*" (See Haggai 2:9.) You and I are part of this coming revival because we are in the "latter-rain" generation. (See, for example, James 5:7.) God wants to pour out His spirit of revival with an awakening on the earth like we have never seen before.

What is revival? Is it necessary? The word *revive* simply means "to restore to life or consciousness." In medical terms, when someone is revived. they are brought back to life again. Many Christians all over the world are in a state of spiritual slumber. Their prayer lives are stagnant, dormant, or even dead. Their love walk has grown cold because their intimacy with God has diminished. If any of the above describes you, you are a prime candidate for revival.

Our churches in America need revival like never before. God is calling the hearts of His people back to Him so we can experience His love and power in our lives. I believe that in conjunction with the revival, we are about to experience the greatest prayer awakening this generation has ever seen. He is raising up intercessors and prophetic leaders all over the world, regardless of culture or denomination. Remember, He said that if we are willing and obedient. we will eat the good of the land. (See Isaiah 1:19.) This verse is not just talking about receiving money or resources, but also about the promise of God to a lost generation. God has promised that in the last days, all will know Him, "*from the least to the greatest.*" (See, for example, Hebrews 8:10–12.) I believe we are living in that very hour. The good news is that God is ready to use anyone who is available to Him. Are you available when God is ready to partner with you to release heaven into the earth?

Day 83: BREAKTHROUGH PRAYER

Father, I thank You for Your spirit of revival and awakening, which You are releasing in the earth right now. I thank You that I am a part of the next move of God in this generation. The next great move will be one of signs, wonders, and miracles in Jesus's name. I surrender my life to You and repent of any spiritual slumber that has been operating in my life. I yield to You and make myself available as a partner in the earth in which Your Spirit can move and flow as You will. I declare that I am a recipient of personal revival and awakening—in my prayer life, in my worship, and in my devotion. Lord, Your Word declares that the glory of the latter house will be greater than the former; therefore, I make myself available to You as a glory carrier. In Jesus's name, amen.

Day 84: Mind Control

Casting down imaginations, and every high thing that exalts itself against the knowledge of God, and bringing into captivity every thought to the obedience of Christ.

(2 Corinthians 10:5)

One of the important elements of supernatural living is the responsibility of taking our thoughts captive *"to the obedience of Christ."* We must renew our minds according to the Word of God. Nothing can substitute for the supernatural power of a transformed mind.

The enemy constantly bombards our minds with thoughts, suggestions, and even arguments that are hostile to the Word of God. But our minds do not have to be the playpen of the devil. Neither do they have to be his dumping ground. We have been empowered to take control of our minds so that our thoughts are aligned with the mind of Christ. That's right, beloved. God has given you the authority to exercise control over your thought life. The Bible says, *"(For the weapons of our warfare are not carnal, but mighty through God to the pulling down of strongholds;) casting down imaginations, and every high thing that exalts itself against the knowledge of God"* (2 Corinthians 10:4–5).

We must learn how to bring our thoughts captive to the obedience of Christ. The best way to get rid of a stronghold is to replace it with another. Thus, we must establish the Word of God as the stronghold in our mind. This is why David declared, *"The name of the LORD is a strong tower: the righteous runs into it, and is safe"* (Proverbs 18:10). Accordingly, the Word of God must be the fortress that we establish in our minds and hearts to evict the thoughts and attitudes of the enemy and erect the thoughts and attitudes of God. Beloved, it is time for you to take control of your mind. No longer allow the reckless thoughts and ideas of the enemy to permeate the atmosphere of your thought life. The Bible tells us that Jesus Himself is the Word of God. (See, for example, John 1:1, 14.) Declare that you have the mind of Christ. The Scripture says, *"You will keep him in perfect peace, whose mind is stayed on You: because he trusts in You"* (Isaiah 26:3). Exercise your spiritual authority today over the thoughts of your mind, and live in victory.

Day 84: BREAKTHROUGH PRAYER

Father, thank You that I have the mind of Christ. I take captive every thought that is hostile to the knowledge of God and bring it into obedience to Christ. I declare that my mind will no longer be the devil's playground. I evict every single thought or suggestion that is demonic or unclean. My mind is holy; therefore, I declare that it is sanctified, in the name of Jesus. Fear, worry, depression, and anxiety have no place there. I declare that my mind is a fortress of purity and righteousness. I command every false and evil thought that has been sent against my mind to be returned to sender. In Jesus's name, amen!

Day 85: Total Restoration

For I will restore health to you, and I will heal you of your wounds, says the Lord; because they called you an outcast, saying, This is Zion, whom no man seeks after.

(Jeremiah 30:17)

The first time I saw my father restore an old junk car in our garage, I was completely amazed. He welded various parts and pieces together, and when he was finished, he drove a functional car out of the garage. It was like a miracle to me. How was he able to do something like that? What ingenuity goes into the process of restoration!

I have said it many times, and I will say again: God is a God of restoration—total restoration. He doesn't do anything incompletely or halfway. The Bible says that He who has begun a good work in us will be faithful to complete it. (See Philippians 1:6.) Have we really understood this truth? God does not start any project that He is incapable of completing. More than that, He actually finishes every project before He starts it. This is difficult for our infinite minds to comprehend, but it makes perfect sense in God's economy. When God took you on as a project, He had every intention of bringing you into the fullness of everything He saw in you before He chose you in Christ in eternity past. (See Ephesians 1:4.) You ought to rejoice—you are in the process of restoration! In Jeremiah 30, God told the Israelites that He would restore health to them. This prophetic declaration was made in the midst of their rebellion and disobedience.

They were facing one of the most devastating seasons of their lives—inevitable destruction and captivity—yet God had a plan to bring them back again. How much more does God desire to restore His children today?

What does total restoration look like? It looks like completeness and wholeness in every area of your life and in the lives of those you care about. It looks like nothing missing and nothing broken. Again, when we experience total restoration, people can't even tell the difficulties we've been through by looking at us. God says He will *"restore to you the years that the locust has eaten"* (Joel 2:25). That's a promise. It doesn't matter what you have been through, restoration is your portion. And not just any restoration—total restoration.

Day 85: BREAKTHROUGH PRAYER

Father, I believe that You are the God of total restoration. I receive Your restoration power right now, in Jesus's name. You promised that You would restore health to me. Every area of rejection, bitterness, brokenness, and barrenness is completely restored by the power of the blood of Jesus and the anointing of the Holy Spirit. Jesus said that He came to *"heal the brokenhearted"* and *"preach the acceptable year of the Lord."* I declare that I am in my jubilee season. All things that were lost to me or defrauded from me must be restored right now. Thank You, Father, for Your goodness and Your grace operating in my life today. I am totally restored. In the name of Jesus, amen. (See Luke 4:18–19; Leviticus 25:1–4, 8–10 NIV.)

Day 86: The Miracle Mandate

Verily, verily, I say to you, he that believes on me, the works that I do shall he do also; and greater works than these shall he do; because I go to My Father. (John 14:12)

I recently heard a message from a minister who stated that miracles do not occur today. At first, I thought this was a laughable teaching, but later I realized there are a number people in the body of Christ who think this way. Many of them do not believe in the operation of the gifts of the Spirit after the time of the apostles.

Yet, if miracles aren't happening today, then this would imply that Jesus is not the same yesterday, today, and forever (see Hebrews 13:8), and that Jesus is not alive and well. Not only do I know that Jesus is alive, but I also know that He wants to manifest His power in and through us today. Do you really believe in miracles? God believes in miracles. The Bible says that the works that Jesus did, we will do also—and even greater works than those.

This is our mandate, beloved: to take the miraculous power of the gospel to a lost and dying generation. Paul wrote in Romans 1:16 that he was not ashamed of the gospel of Christ, because he recognized that it was the power of God for salvation. The Greek word translated *"power"* in that verse is *dunamis,* which, as we have seen, refers to miracle-working power. In other words, the gospel contains a miracle-working power. Any gospel that does not display the miraculous power of God is not the true gospel. In the Western world, we seem to have a problem with over-intellectualizing. We tend to believe that if we can't figure something out through reason, it must be invalid. But the Bible says, "*God has chosen the foolish things of the world to confound the wise*" (1 Corinthians 1:27). Will you be simple enough to believe that God is exactly who He says He is? Do you possess a childlike faith that believes in miracles? Our mandate is to bring the supernatural power of God to the nations of the earth, through the gospel of Jesus Christ. We serve a risen Savior who has released the power of the resurrection. As His follower, are you ready to release His power today?

Day 86: BREAKTHROUGH PRAYER

Father, thank You for Your miraculous power working in my life. I receive the miracle mandate to take the gospel to the nations. I thank You for confirming Your Word with signs, wonders, and miracles in Jesus's name. I release my faith in the power of the Holy Spirit, and I posture myself to partner with heaven as an ambassador of the kingdom of God. Demonstrate Your love, Father, by healing the sick, casting out demons, and raising the dead by my hands. I give my body to You as a vessel of honor; do with it as You will. I surrender myself to You so that I may walk in the miraculous daily. Signs, wonders, and miracles are a normal part of my everyday life. Today, I embrace a supernatural lifestyle as a part of the Great Commission of Jesus Christ. Use me to touch someone's life in a miraculous way. In Jesus's name, amen. (See Mark 16:20; 2 Timothy 2:21.)

Day 87: Speak the Word

The centurion answered and said, Lord, I am not worthy that You should come under my roof: but speak the word only, and my servant shall be healed. (Matthew 8:8)

I have said on many occasions that one of the most underestimated spiritual principles is the power of our words. The record of the Bible is clear that "*death and life are in the power of the tongue*" (Proverbs 18:21). The centurion in the gospel of Matthew understood the power and authority of the spoken word. Because he was a man of authority, he understood the procedure that when you spoke something to those under you, it should come to pass.

Consider various areas of your life. How many times have you been affected by words that someone has spoken? The reality is that if we would learn to speak God's Word in faith, we would see tremendous change and transformation in our lives. This has been a recurring theme in this devotional, and it can't be emphasized enough. The problem is that people don't often read and meditate on God's Word, let alone speak it. Psalm 107:20 says that God "*sent His word, and healed them, and delivered them from their destructions.*"

As we have seen, one word can transform a life. Like the centurion, God wants us to understand that if we need a miracle, we must learn to declare His Word. The centurion's servant was healed, even though Jesus never touched him physically, because of the power of the word of God. Remember that when

God created the universe, He spoke it into being by His words. That same creative power lives in you by the Holy Spirit. Jesus said that we will have what we say. (See Mark 11:23–24.) Is it that simple? Yes! Challenge yourself today to speak only the Word of God. Don't speak your opinions, your frustrations, or your fears—speak the Word only. The centurion told Jesus that if He would only speak the word, his servant would be healed. Is that your confession of faith today? "Lord, all I need is one word from You to bring healing, deliverance, and breakthrough in my life." Open your mouth and declare breakthrough right now.

Day 87: BREAKTHROUGH PRAYER

Father, thank You for the power of Your words. Your words created the natural world. You spoke into the darkness and said, "*Let there be light.*" Therefore, I speak into the darkness and say, "Light, be." "*In the beginning was the Word, and the Word was with God, and the Word was God.... All things were made by Him; and without Him was not any thing made that was made.*" I declare that my world is framed by the *rhema* word of God. Release healing and deliverance through my mouth, in Jesus's name. I declare that Your Word is truth. Nothing is impossible to me because I believe Your Word. I use my words as a spiritual weapon to dismantle the kingdom of darkness and the lies of the enemy that have operated in my life. I declare that I am free from all bondage and shackles. I speak Your Word only, and I receive my miracle today. In Jesus's name, amen. (See Genesis 1:3; John 1:1, 3; John 17:17.)

Day 88: Your Season of Promotion

For promotion comes neither from the east, nor from the west, nor from the south. But God is the judge: He puts down one, and sets up another. (Psalm 75:6–7)

I remember when social media first came out. It was an overnight success. Millions of people from all over the world were able to connect instantly. Unfortunately, one of the consequences of social media has been massive self-promotion. It has become a means of advertising people, products, services, even ministries. There is nothing wrong with advertisement, in itself, but we must be careful not to fall into the dangerous trap of constantly promoting ourselves for self-centered purposes.

The writer of Psalm 75 said that promotion doesn't come from the east, the west, or the south but from the Lord. (See verses 6–7.) That's right, God is your promoter. Do you know what that means? It means you never have to rely upon self-promotion to get where God has called you to be. I am reminded of the famous promoter Don King. He was such a skilled communicator that he could sell a shell to a turtle. He promoted the "Rumble in the Jungle," the famous boxing match in the 1970s between George Foreman and Muhammad Ali. If such promotion by natural man could go down in history, how much more the promotion of God!

You are entering into a season of the greatest promotion in your life. God is about to open doors for you that no one can close. (See Isaiah 22:22.) It doesn't matter what your education or affiliation is—if you will trust in the mighty hand of God, you will see promotion. God is about to radically reshape your life to His glory. Get ready. Get in position. Don't be either discouraged or impatient. God has something so good for you that you wouldn't be able to dream it up. You are about to be celebrated like never before. Your season of jubilation has come. Your season of promotion is now.

Day 88: BREAKTHROUGH PRAYER

Father, in the name of Jesus, I thank You for who You are and all that You have done in my life. I declare that Your Word is like a hammer that breaks rock in pieces. Your Word has made a way for me. You have opened doors for me that no one can close. You have lifted my head above all my enemies around me. You said in Your Word that if we would humble ourselves, You would exalt us in due season. I declare that my due season is upon me. I declare that my season of elevation is now. I declare that my season of celebration is now. I declare that unusual favor is operating in my life. I declare that destiny-helpers are being mobilized and activated to assist me. Good things are happening in my life. Miracles are coming into manifestation. Just as Joseph moved from the pit to the palace, I have moved from the pit of despair to the palace of promotion. In the mighty name of Jesus, amen. (See Jeremiah 23:29; Psalm 27:6; 1 Peter 5:6.)

Day 89: The Power of Covenant

But with you will I establish My covenant; and you shall come into the ark, you, and your sons, and your wife, and your sons' wives with you. (Genesis 6:18)

In a theological sense, the definition of *covenant* is "an agreement which brings about a relationship of commitment between God and his people." God is a covenantal God. Throughout the Bible, we see that the Lord speaks to His people in terms of covenant, yet most believers are ignorant of the spiritual ramifications of a covenantal relationship. The more we understand covenant, the more we understand God, and the more we understand God, the more we understand covenant. Everything about our relationship with God is based upon covenant.

One of the problems we have in our contemporary world is that we tend to be a society of covenant-breakers. That is why, if we look at God through the lens of our earthly culture, we will misunderstand the power of His promises. Beloved, God cannot lie. When He says He is going to heal you, it is because He is the Healer. When He says He is going to deliver you, it is because He is the Deliverer. The psalmist says about God, "*You have magnified Your word above all Your name*" (Psalm 138:2). His word is His bond. If He says it, that settles it.

In ancient days, when men made a covenant between one another, they would swear by someone greater than themselves. The Bible says that when God made a covenant with Abraham, He could not swear by anyone greater than Himself.

(See Hebrews 6:13.) Why? Because there is no one greater than God! Covenant was also binding unto death. Thus, when God made a blood covenant with us through Jesus Christ, He came into an oath with Himself concerning us. This is why the Word of God says that whoever calls on the name of the Lord will be saved, or delivered. (See, for example, Romans 10:13.) We can call on Him because we have a covenantal relationship with Him through Jesus. The blood of Jesus was the payment, the legal tender, for this covenant we have with God. The more you understand this concept, the more you will live a life of breakthrough and freedom. It's not about you—it's about Him. As I have expressed previously when describing God's blessings and benefits, any covenantal rights you fail to claim are covenantal rights you fail to enjoy. Release your faith in your covenant God today!

Day 89: BREAKTHROUGH PRAYER

Father, in the name of Jesus, I thank You that You are a covenantal God. You are bound to Your Word, and You cannot lie. What You have spoken will surely come to pass. What You have promised, You are faithful to perform. Because of the integrity of Your Word, I can rest assured that what You have spoken will surely come into manifestation in my life. I place my confidence in Your Word today, and I declare that what You have spoken is the absolute truth. Lord, You said in Your Word that You would never leave me or forsake me; therefore, I stand upon that promise. I am never alone, and I will never be alone, in Jesus's name. You are the Prince of Peace. Therefore, anxiety has no place in my heart or mind. Thank You for the manifestation of Your goodness in my life. Thank You for Your great grace, whereby You have saved and delivered me from the bondage of sin. Lord, You are good, and Your mercy endures forever! In Jesus's name, amen. (See Hebrews 10:23; Hebrews 13:5; Psalm 100:5; 106:1; 118:29.)

Day 90: Times of Refreshing

Repent you therefore, and be converted, that your sins may be blotted out, when the times of refreshing shall come from the presence of the Lord. (Acts 3:19)

Growing up, I used to play outside on hot summer days, and then I would drink lemonade or sweet tea to cool off. Those drinks might not have been healthy, but they were very refreshing! Think about a time when you were outside on a warm day, and then you drank something cool and refreshing. How did you react to it? You probably took a deep breath and exhaled strongly. These are examples of taking enjoyment from natural refreshment, but there is a spiritual refreshment that is far greater. The Bible says that if we will repent, we will receive *"times of refreshing...from the presence of the Lord."* Are you weary? Are you burdened? It's time for you to be refreshed by God's presence.

"Repent you therefore, and be converted." Repentance is more than just sorrow. In fact, in the Greek, the word *"repent"* here means "to change one's mind for the better." If we will change our mind so that it is aligned with God's Word and ways, we will be refreshed. Jesus told His disciples that His yoke was easy and His burden was light. (See Matthew 11:30.) Are you carrying a burden in your life? It is time for you to cast your burden on Him because He cares for you. (See 1 Peter 5:7.)

One of the fundamental keys of breakthrough is looking at situations and circumstances from the right vantage point.

Throughout this book, we have seen many examples of people who tapped into God's supernatural power by faith and defied the odds. They were willing to look beyond what they saw in the natural and see God's infinite plan and potential for their lives. The same is true of us, beloved. If you will dare to change the way you think so that it matches God's Word, and look at things from a heavenly perspective, you will receive your miracle. Don't be exhausted by negativity. Don't be wearied by anxiety. Don't allow the circumstances of your life to manipulate you. Receive the refreshing touch of the Lord today. The Holy Spirit is here—drink deeply from Him. It is time for you to be restored, in the name of Jesus.

Day 90: BREAKTHROUGH PRAYER

> Father, I receive Your supernatural refreshment from Your presence. Holy Spirit, I ask You to come and move in the miraculous. Thank You for being the God of restoration. Thank You for restoring the years that the enemy has stolen away. Thank You for releasing breakthrough in my life. I declare that my mind is renewed, my body is healed, and my soul is restored. I am refreshed in peace and joy, freed from all anxiety and fear. I declare that I will never be anxious again. I will never be bound by fear. Father, I acknowledge the rejuvenating power of Your Spirit flowing in me right now. Thank You, Holy Spirit, for refreshing me today. In Jesus's name, amen!

About the Author

Pastor Kynan T. Bridges is the senior pastor of Grace & Peace Global Fellowship in Tampa, Florida. Through his profound revelation of the Word of God and his dynamic teaching ministry, Pastor Bridges has revolutionized the lives of many in the body of Christ. Through his practical approach to applying the deep truths of the Word of God, he reveals the authority and identity of the new covenant believer.

God has placed on Pastor Kynan a peculiar anointing for understanding and teaching the Scriptures, along with the gift of prophecy and healing. Pastor Kynan and his wife, Gloria, through an apostolic anointing, are committed to equipping the body of Christ to live in the supernatural every day and to fulfill the Great Commission. It is the desire of Pastor Kynan to see the nations transformed by the unconditional love of God.

A highly sought speaker, Pastor Kynan is a prolific author. His books with Whitaker House include *90 Days of Breakthrough, Overcoming Familiar Spirits, 30 Prayers of Divine Protection, Unlocking the Code of the Supernatural, School of the Miraculous, Invading the Heavens, Unmasking the Accuser, Kingdom Authority,* and *Power of Prophetic Prayer.*

Pastor Kynan is also a committed husband to Gloria, a mentor, and the father of five beautiful children: Ella, Naomi, Isaac, Israel, and Anna.